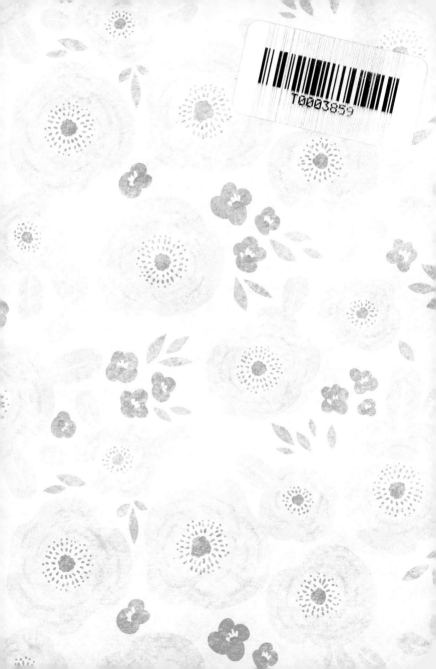

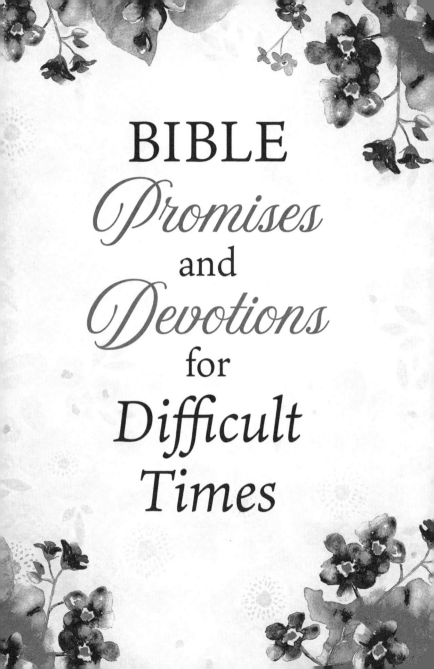

BIBLE
Promises
and
Devotions
for
Difficult
Times

BIBLE
Promises
and
Devotions
for
Difficult
Times

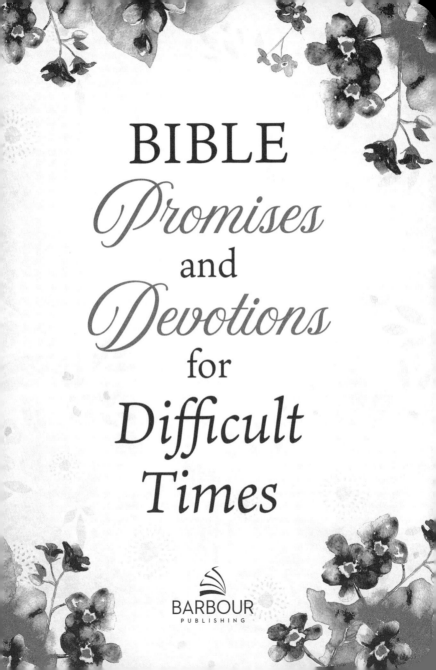

BARBOUR
PUBLISHING

Contents

Introduction

Jesus said, "Here on earth you will have many trials and sorrows." It's a promise: you can expect suffering during your lifetime. Jesus went on to say, "But take heart, because I have overcome the world" (John 16:33 NLT). This is good news, but it doesn't necessarily mean the Lord will quickly resolve any difficulties you encounter.

What He offers is not a problem-free life, but the strength to endure your burdens and overcome your tests. Christians today are not spared many of the griefs that assail humanity—including financial pressures, bankruptcies, dysfunctional relationships, marital breakups, accidents, and diseases. This is why God gave us His Word, "that we through the patience and comfort of the Scriptures might have hope" (Romans 15:4 NKJV).

Bible Promises and Devotions for Difficult Times draws from these deep wells of encouragement. It was written to breathe life into you when you are forced to walk a very difficult path. It doesn't offer simplistic answers to serious problems, but it does offer hope—real hope—for your darkest hours.

This devotional declares boldly that God will never, ever forsake you, even when your way seems impossible, your circumstances seem unbearable, and you are most tempted to despair. May you find hope in these pages.

Abuse

Abuse is a topic that's hard to talk about openly. Whether it's something that lies long ago in our past or something we are dealing with in the present, the shame that often goes along with abuse is hard to face.

But God wants to take away that sense of shame. Abuse tells lies. It says that the abused person is unworthy of love and dignity and respect. God longs to smash those lies with the love and truth of Christ's Gospel.

He is waiting to help us walk away from abuse—into a new life.

Drive out a scoffer, and strife will go out,
and quarreling and abuse will cease.
PROVERBS 22:10 ESV

The LORD is a God who avenges.
O God who avenges, shine forth.
PSALM 94:1 NIV

"Bless those who curse you, pray for those who abuse you."
LUKE 6:28 ESV

He saves me from those who hate me. Yes,
You lift me above those who rise up against me.
You save me from those who want to hurt me.
PSALM 18:48 NLV

For he has not despised or scorned the suffering of
the afflicted one; he has not hidden his face from
him but has listened to his cry for help.
PSALM 22:24 NIV

Repay no one evil for evil. Have regard for good things in the sight of all men. If it is possible, as much as depends on you, live peaceably with all men. Beloved, do not avenge yourselves, but rather give place to wrath; for it is written, "Vengeance is Mine, I will repay," says the Lord. . . . Do not be overcome by evil, but overcome evil with good.

ROMANS 12:17–19, 21 NKJV

"Their anger will be punished, for it is bad. Their bad temper will be punished, for it is bad. I will divide them in Jacob and spread them apart in Israel."

GENESIS 49:7 NLV

"If you hurt my daughters, or if you take wives other than my daughters, no man may see it. But God sees what happens between you and me."

GENESIS 31:50 NLV

But you, God, see the trouble of the afflicted; you consider their grief and take it in hand. The victims commit themselves to you; you are the helper of the fatherless. Break the arm of the wicked man; call the evildoer to account for his wickedness that would not otherwise be found out.

PSALM 10:14–15 NIV

He shall redeem their soul from deceit and violence:
and precious shall their blood be in his sight.
PSALM 72:14 KJV

The LORD is good, a refuge in times of trouble.
He cares for those who trust in him.
NAHUM 1:7 NIV

Those who sow with tears will reap with songs of joy.
PSALM 126:5 NIV

The Spirit himself testifies with our spirit that we are God's
children. Now if we are children, then we are heirs—heirs
of God and co-heirs with Christ, if indeed we share in his
sufferings in order that we may also share in his glory.
ROMANS 8:16–17 NIV

Record my misery; list my tears on your scroll—are they not
in your record? Then my enemies will turn back when I call
for help. By this I will know that God is for me. In God,
whose word I praise, in the LORD, whose word I praise—
in God I trust and am not afraid. What can man do to me?
PSALM 56:8–11 NIV

Therefore, if anyone is in Christ, the new creation
has come: The old has gone, the new is here!
2 CORINTHIANS 5:17 NIV

Strengthen the hands which hang down, and the feeble knees.
HEBREWS 12:12 NKJV

*And the afflicted people thou wilt save: but thine eyes are
upon the haughty, that thou mayest bring them down.*
2 SAMUEL 22:28 KJV

*The LORD also will be a refuge for the
oppressed, a refuge in times of trouble.*
PSALM 9:9 NKJV

*"Broken bone for broken bone, eye for eye, tooth for
tooth. Just as he has hurt a man, so he will be hurt."*
LEVITICUS 24:20 NLV

*Pleasing words are like honey. They are sweet
to the soul and healing to the bones.*
PROVERBS 16:24 NLV

---

*Jesus, I know You came to heal the brokenhearted. Heal
my broken heart, I pray. You came to deliver captives into
freedom. Set me free from abuse. You came to heal those who
are bruised. I ask that You heal the scars of abuse in my heart,
in my mind and memories, and in my life. Please rescue me!*

CLOSE TO HIS HEART

He tends his flock like a shepherd: He gathers the lambs
in his arms and carries them close to his heart.

ISAIAH 40:11 NIV

When the disciples tried to keep children away from Jesus, He said, "Let the little children come to me" (Mark 10:14 NIV). He then took them in His arms and blessed them. Gathering the lambs in His arms has always been Jesus' way.

But if you have suffered abuse or neglect, gone hungry, or experienced trauma, you may wonder where the Lord was. And where is He now? The Bible assures you: "The LORD is close to the brokenhearted" (Psalm 34:18 NIV). God sees your pain. He loves you and cares deeply for you.

Whatever anyone has done to you, they have done to Jesus (Matthew 25:34–45), so He empathizes with your suffering. "In all their suffering he also suffered" (Isaiah 63:9 NLT). This is one reason Jesus was called "a man of sorrows, and acquainted with grief" (Isaiah 53:3 KJV).

God not only knows when you experience grief, but He feels your pain and is there to comfort you if you will let Him.

RECOVERING FROM ABUSE

"O you afflicted one, tossed with tempest, and not comforted. . . .
You shall be far from oppression, for you shall not fear."
ISAIAH 54:11, 14 NKJV

In these verses, God speaks to an afflicted person who has suffered from oppressors. Then He describes how she will be rebuilt with precious stones like a beautiful spiritual city (vv. 11–12). The imagery God invokes is strikingly similar to the heavenly Jerusalem in Revelation 21–22, and the similarity is intentional.

Have you suffered abuse in some form? Are you unable to find lasting comfort? Know that God can help you to gain victory over trauma, and He longs for you to experience peace. You can begin to enjoy a foretaste of heaven here and now.

God is able to restore your life and to build you up spiritually so that you will be strong and radiant. Allow His Holy Spirit to enter the darkest corners of your memories, wash away the fear, and cleanse you from guilt, anger, and insecurity.

Recovering from abuse can take years, but God can throw aside the curtains in sudden moments of revelation and splash His sunlight in your soul.

GOD SEES YOUR PLIGHT

The Egyptians abused and battered us,
in a cruel and savage slavery.
DEUTERONOMY 26:6 MSG

Women trapped in abusive relationships and children from dysfunctional families can identify with those words, "abused and battered," yet they describe the desperate plight of God's people in Egypt thirty-five hundred years ago.

The next verse says, "We cried out to GOD. . .He listened to our voice, he saw our destitution, our trouble, our cruel plight" (Deuteronomy 26:7 MSG). "The Israelites groaned in their slavery and cried out, and their cry for help. . .went up to God" (Exodus 2:23 NIV). God heard them and set them free.

God knows the suffering you have endured, He hears your prayers, and His heart is moved. He will take steps to deliver you from your plight and to comfort you.

He is with you, even in the silence and loneliness, and in your darkest moments when you feel the most damaged and worthless, He looks on you as His own child, of inestimable worth. One day you will meet Him face to face and He will wipe all tears from your eyes (Revelation 7:17). In the meantime, He is always with you, comforting you.

OVERCOMING THE PAST

"You make victims of the children and leave them vulnerable to violence and vice."

MICAH 2:9 MSG

Frequently, children who are victims of abuse, violence, or neglect grow up insecure and, in later years, look for approval and acceptance in the wrong places. They may seek solace in alcohol or drugs, or they may search for fulfillment in unhealthy relationships, where they are vulnerable to further violence and vice.

You really have to admire those who had traumatic childhoods and yet are resolving and overcoming their issues to find wholeness and fulfillment. But it is not easy. God offers healing, but it takes a determination to rise above the past, to close the door to anger, and to build a new life in Christ.

"If anyone is in Christ, he is a new creation; old things have passed away; behold, all things have become new" (2 Corinthians 5:17 NKJV). God does a major work in people's heart at salvation, but complete transformation takes a lifetime. "We. . .beholding as in a mirror the glory of the Lord, are being transformed into the same image" (2 Corinthians 3:18 NKJV).

It takes time, but we are being transformed.

Accidents

When an accident happens, we're suddenly struck with how fragile our lives are. Our sense of safety and security shatters. Life feels shaky, as though unexpected danger lurks around every corner. It's hard to regain a sense of peace.

But the same divine energy that made the world is still at work in each and every event of our lives. What seems like catastrophe will be swept up by God's power and made into something that will bless us and those we love.

True faith means we trust God to use even the bad things for our good and His glory.

And we know that in all things God works for the good of those who love him, who have been called according to his purpose.

ROMANS 8:28 NIV

God is our refuge and strength, a very present help in trouble. Therefore we will not fear though the earth gives way, though the mountains be moved into the heart of the sea, though its waters roar and foam, though the mountains tremble at its swelling.

PSALM 46:1–3 ESV

The LORD shall preserve thee from all evil: he shall preserve thy soul. The LORD shall preserve thy going out and thy coming in from this time forth, and even for evermore.

PSALM 121:7–8 KJV

Of Benjamin he said: "The beloved of the LORD shall dwell in safety by Him, who shelters him all the day long; and he shall dwell between His shoulders."

DEUTERONOMY 33:12 NKJV

He shall cover thee with his feathers, and under his wings shalt thou trust: his truth shall be thy shield and buckler.

PSALM 91:4 KJV

I have been in danger from rivers, in danger from bandits, in danger from my fellow Jews, in danger from Gentiles; in danger in the city, in danger in the country, in danger at sea. . . . Three times I pleaded with the Lord to take [the thorn in my flesh] away from me. But he said to me, "My grace is sufficient for you."

2 CORINTHIANS 11:26; 12:8–9 NIV

You who fear the LORD, trust in the LORD! He is their help and their shield.

PSALM 115:11 ESV

You are my strength, I watch for you; you, God, are my fortress, my God on whom I can rely. God will go before me.

PSALM 59:9–10 NIV

Only God can say what is right or wrong. . . . He can save or put to death. . . . Listen! You who say, "Today or tomorrow we will go to this city and stay a year and make money." You do not know about tomorrow. What is your life? It is like fog. You see it and soon it is gone. What you should say is, "If the Lord wants us to, we will live and do this or that."

JAMES 4:12–15 NLV

"Blessed are the poor in spirit, for theirs is the kingdom of heaven."

MATTHEW 5:3 NIV

Who shall separate us from the love of Christ?
Shall trouble or hardship or persecution or
famine or nakedness or danger or sword?
ROMANS 8:35 NIV

*"The L*ORD *himself goes before you and will be with*
you; he will never leave you nor forsake you."
DEUTERONOMY 31:8 NIV

"For I know the plans I have for you," says the Lord, "plans for
well-being and not for trouble, to give you a future and a hope."
JEREMIAH 29:11 NLV

Though I walk in the midst of trouble, You will
revive me. . .Your right hand will save me.
PSALM 138:7 NKJV

"When the earth totters, and all its inhabitants,
it is I who keep steady its pillars."
PSALM 75:3 ESV

We do not look at the things that can be seen. We look at the
things that cannot be seen. The things that can be seen will come
to an end. But the things that cannot be seen will last forever.
2 CORINTHIANS 4:18 NLV

Be thou my strong habitation, whereunto I may continually resort: thou hast given commandment to save me; for thou art my rock and my fortress.

PSALM 71:3 KJV

He who lives in the safe place of the Most High will be in the shadow of the All-powerful. I will say to the Lord, "You are my safe and strong place, my God."

PSALM 91:1–2 NLV

God, my world seems upside down.
And yet I trust You.
The timing couldn't be worse.
And yet I trust You.
I am overwhelmed with emotion
and weariness as I try to
deal with these events.
And yet I trust You.

OCCUPATIONAL HAZARDS

When you chop wood, there is danger
with each stroke of your ax.
ECCLESIASTES 10:9 NLT

When you are injured on the job, you are filled with conflicting thoughts. On the one hand, you know that all occupations have hazards. Soldiers, policemen, and firemen are aware that their jobs are dangerous, but even desk jobs have liabilities.

Still, you may wonder, "Why didn't God protect me?" After all, the Bible promises, "If you. . .make the Most High your dwelling, no harm will overtake you, no disaster will come near your tent. For he will command his angels concerning you to guard you in all your ways" (Psalm 91:9–11 NIV).

Staying close to God definitely guards you from a great deal of misfortune, but the fact is, it won't guarantee you a completely trouble-free existence. The Bible states, "People are born for trouble as readily as sparks fly up from a fire" (Job 5:7 NLT). That's the way life is. We all get sick. We all feel pain. We all have accidents.

But the good news is: "There is wonderful joy ahead, even though you must endure many trials for a little while" (1 Peter 1:6 NLT).

UNEXPECTED INJURIES

Ahaziah had fallen through the lattice of his upper
room in Samaria and injured himself.

2 KINGS 1:2 NIV

In Bible times, people covered their window openings with thin slats of wood called latticework. One day King Ahaziah was in an upper palace room and leaned heavily against the latticework, causing it to break. He plunged to the courtyard below and was seriously injured (2 Kings 1:2). Because he looked to the false god Baal-Zebub for healing, he died (vv. 16–17).

You may trust in God, but that is not a guarantee that you will never have an accident. The difference is that God constantly works on behalf of His children to bring great good out of tragedies. "All things work together for good to those who love God" (Romans 8:28 NKJV), even accidents.

When you suffer unexpected misfortune, God can see to it that you also experience unexpected good as a result—benefits such as spiritual depth, compassion, and patience.

You might rather do without spiritual benefits and simply enjoy a trouble-free, easy life, but God is seeking to transform you into a better person, and to do so, He often has to bring you through troubled times.

UNEXPLAINED MISFORTUNE

No one can predict misfortune. . . So men and women are caught by accidents evil and sudden.

ECCLESIASTES 9:12 MSG

Many Christians believe that nothing happens randomly. They insist that God is in control of events down to the very tiniest details. And since He is able to protect them from all accidents and misfortune, when accidents happen God must have good reasons for allowing them, even if these reasons aren't apparent.

This is true, but to focus on that is to miss the big picture. God is definitely able to micromanage events in believers' lives to bring about His purposes, but it is important to realize that He is focused on the larger issues. The psalmist said of God, "Your thoughts are very deep" (Psalm 92:5 NKJV).

Some people demand, "Why, God?" They insist that God explain His actions. They desire an itemized justification for every injury He allowed. Meanwhile, God's concern is the overall condition of their heart. He is watching whether they will trust Him no matter what.

The fact is, most times in this life you won't understand why God has allowed an accident. So focus on what's most important—loving Him and remaining true to Him through it all.

GUARDED FROM EVIL

*They will lift you up in their hands, so that you
will not strike your foot against a stone.*

PSALM 91:12 NIV

You may be confused when reading the promises of Psalm 91. Verse 11 (NIV) says that God's angels will "guard you in all your ways." The very next verse promises that they won't even allow you to stub your toe against a stone. However, you know from experience that you and most other believers do suffer injury from time to time, sometimes even serious injuries.

Yet the Psalm promises, "No harm will overtake you" (v. 10 NIV). It sounds like you should expect to experience a totally blessed, trouble-free life. So what gives?

The answer is that this is the ideal state, promised when you passionately love God and know Him (v. 14). The opening verse states that these promises are for "whoever dwells in the shelter of the Most High" (v. 1). You must *constantly* dwell close to God's heart, sheltered by His presence.

Most Christians don't abide that close to God. So although He still protects you, often in direct correlation to how close you are to Him, you will occasionally suffer accidents.

ACCIDENTS AND JUDGMENT

"What about the eighteen people who died when the tower in Siloam fell on them? Were they the worst sinners in Jerusalem?"

LUKE 13:4 NLT

Many Jews believed there were no such things as "accidents." Whenever something bad happened to someone, it was considered God's judgment on sin.

But at a certain level, this rationale breaks down. After all, carpenters use sharp tools to cut wood and end up with nicks and cuts fairly frequently (Ecclesiastes 10:9). So only the *biggest* accidents were considered judgments—but even so, this isn't a cause-and-effect rule that applies in every case.

Proverbs 26:27 (NKJV) says, "He who rolls a stone will have it roll back on him," so when eighteen people were killed by collapsing stones, many Jews were absolutely convinced that those men had been the worst sinners in the city. But Jesus disputed this.

He said that those men had been no worse than the people standing around pointing their fingers. They all were sinners, so it could have happened to any of them (Luke 13:5). Now, God sometimes does judge sin by allowing accidents, but only He knows each situation, so let's stop judging others.

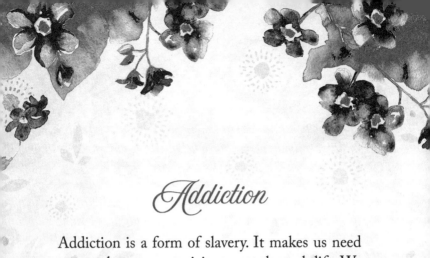

Addiction

Addiction is a form of slavery. It makes us need some substance or activity to get through life. We may not realize how big the problem is, but sooner or later, we wake up to the fact that addiction has become the master. No matter what we believe intellectually about God, addiction becomes our real god. We no longer rely on the Creator of the universe for help with life's challenges. Instead, we cannot face stress or sorrow, weariness or anger, without turning to our addiction.

But God wants to set us free. Jesus came to break the bonds of slavery—including the slavery of addiction!

It is for freedom that Christ has set us free. Stand firm, then, and do not let yourselves be burdened again by a yoke of slavery.
GALATIANS 5:1 NIV

For I know that in me (that is, in my flesh) nothing good dwells; for to will is present with me, but how to perform what is good I do not find. For the good that I will to do, I do not do; but the evil I will not to do, that I practice. Now if I do what I will not to do, it is no longer I who do it, but sin that dwells in me. . . . O wretched man that I am! Who will deliver me from this body of death? I thank God—through Jesus Christ our Lord!
ROMANS 7:18–20, 24–25 NKJV

Peter said to them, "Be sorry for your sins and turn from them and be baptized in the name of Jesus Christ, and your sins will be forgiven. You will receive the gift of the Holy Spirit."
ACTS 2:38 NLV

The Spirit of the Lord GOD is upon me, because the LORD has anointed me to bring good news to the poor; he has sent me to bind up the brokenhearted, to proclaim liberty to the captives, and the opening of the prison to those who are bound.
ISAIAH 61:1 ESV

*I can do all this through him
who gives me strength.*
PHILIPPIANS 4:13 NIV

*God is faithful. He will not allow you to be
tempted more than you can take. But when you
are tempted, He will make a way for you.*
1 CORINTHIANS 10:13 NLV

*The creation itself will be set free from its bondage to corruption
and obtain the freedom of the glory of the children of God.*
ROMANS 8:21 ESV

*Be sober-minded; be watchful. Your adversary the devil
prowls around like a roaring lion, seeking someone to devour.
Resist him, firm in your faith, knowing that the same kinds of
suffering are being experienced by your brotherhood throughout
the world. And after you have suffered a little while, the God
of all grace, who has called you to his eternal glory in Christ,
will himself restore, confirm, strengthen, and establish you.*
1 PETER 5:8–10 ESV

*Thanks be to God, who delivers me
through Jesus Christ our Lord!*
ROMANS 7:25 NIV

So then, Christian brothers, we are not to do what our sinful old selves want us to do. If you do what your sinful old selves want you to do, you will die in sin. But if, through the power of the Holy Spirit, you destroy those actions to which the body can be led, you will have life. All those who are led by the Holy Spirit are sons of God.
ROMANS 8:12–14 NLV

Get your minds ready for good use. Keep awake. Set your hope now and forever on the loving-favor to be given you when Jesus Christ comes again.
1 PETER 1:13 NLV

Confess your faults one to another, and pray one for another, that ye may be healed. The effectual fervent prayer of a righteous man availeth much.
JAMES 5:16 KJV

God bought you with a great price. So honor God with your body. You belong to Him.
1 CORINTHIANS 6:20 NLV

*I say then: Walk in the Spirit, and you
shall not fulfill the lust of the flesh.*
GALATIANS 5:16 NKJV

*For if a man belongs to Christ, he is a new person.
The old life is gone. New life has begun.*
2 CORINTHIANS 5:17 NLV

*"Therefore if the Son makes you free,
you shall be free indeed."*
JOHN 8:36 NKJV

*But may all who seek you rejoice and be glad
in you; may those who long for your saving
help always say, "The LORD is great!"*
PSALM 40:16 NIV

---

*Lord, You know I want to change. And yet again and
again, I fall back into the same addictive behaviors.
I get so discouraged with myself. Thank You, Lord,
that You are never discouraged with me. You are
always waiting to give me one more chance.*

CAUGHT IN A VICIOUS CYCLE

A man of great wrath shall suffer punishment:
for if thou deliver him, yet thou must do it again.

PROVERBS 19:19 KJV

When you have an addiction, you find yourself compulsively indulging in harmful behavior, even though you know it is destructive. This is true for those prone to anger, but it is also true if your addiction is gambling, overeating, pornography, spending, or alcohol.

Someone may mercifully step in and deliver you from the mess you make of your life and cushion the consequences of your actions, but does that really help? They will just have to do it again next week.

If you have an addiction, Paul's words describe your dilemma: "I obviously need help!. . . I can will it, but I can't do it. I decide to do good, but I don't really do it; I decide not to do bad, but then I do it anyway. . . . Is there no one who can do anything for me?. . . The answer, thank God, is that Jesus Christ can and does" (Romans 7:18–19, 24–25 MSG).

When you finally come to the end of yourself, you are ready for God's solution.

LUST AND PORNOGRAPHY

*"I have made a covenant with my eyes; why
then should I look upon a young woman?"*

JOB 31:1 NKJV

Many men are addicted to pornography. It starts "harmlessly." They allow their eyes to linger a few seconds on attractive women—in person or in the media—while entertaining fleeting thoughts of sexual pleasure. If they make little effort to resist such thoughts, they become more frequent. Eventually, they begin visiting explicit websites.

They can become addicted to the rushes of excitement, which are, however, followed by guilt and a weakened prayer life. Paul promises, "No temptation has overtaken you except such as is common to man; but God. . .will also make the way of escape, that you may be able to bear it" (1 Corinthians 10:13 NKJV).

Four thousand years ago, Job said, "I have made a covenant with my eyes" (Job 31:1 NKJV). Job knew he had to nip lust in the bud. So he made a firm decision not to allow his eyes to linger on a young woman, not to indulge in even a fleeting lust.

He stopped lust cold—and it kept him from a great deal of trouble.

STUCK IN THE MUD

*"A sow that is washed returns to
her wallowing in the mud."*
2 PETER 2:22 NIV

One of the most frustrating things about an addiction is that even though you recognize that it is wreaking havoc in your life, and you make a decision to stop it, it often has such a powerful grip that before you know it, you are at it again.

Although it isn't flattering to envision yourself like a pig rolling in the mud, it may be helpful to look at your addiction in light of this statement. The point of the word picture is that simply attempting to clean up your act on the outside isn't enough. Until you have a change in your basic nature, you will continually return to your addiction after attempts to stop.

That is why you need the life-changing power of the Holy Spirit to take hold of your mind and spirit and bring about lasting change. This usually takes time, and it will certainly take repeated, desperate prayers. You have to really want change, doggedly pursue God, and not give up until He answers your prayers.

Fortunately, God continually gives you another chance, even after you mess up again.

ADDICTED TO PLEASURE

You're addicted to thrills? What an empty life!
The pursuit of pleasure is never satisfied.
PROVERBS 21:17 MSG

Addictions come in many forms. Some people are addicted to nonprescription drugs. Many people are addicted to the love hormones, dopamine and norepinephrine, and constantly seek thrills from illicit sexual encounters. They "live for lustful pleasure" (Ephesians 4:19 NLT). Some people's brains release dopamine when they are engaged in extreme sports. They receive a pleasurable reward from high-risk activities and so repeatedly come back for more.

But whether the thrills people pursue are illegal, immoral, or simply insanely dangerous, the Bible says that the constant pursuit of pleasure is never satisfied. A life lived only for selfish pleasure and fulfillment is empty, and it often becomes expensive very quickly. "Those who love pleasure become poor; those who love wine and luxury will never be rich" (Proverbs 21:17 NLT).

People are addicted to things and substances for the rewards they give them. If you want to break free from such addictions and truly enjoy life, you have to find fulfillment in God. "In Your presence is fullness of joy; at Your right hand are pleasures forevermore" (Psalm 16:11 NKJV).

DEFILING GOD'S TEMPLE

If anyone defiles the temple of God, God will destroy him.
For the temple of God is holy, which temple you are.
1 CORINTHIANS 3:17 NKJV

At first drugs are an exciting thrill. You never knew you could experience such things—the stresses and boredom of your daily life seem a million miles away. And the fact that they are illegal sometimes makes them seem even more desirable.

But drugs have a harsh long-term effect on your mind and body. The ecstasy you enjoy comes with an excessively high price tag. After a while, you need greater doses to achieve the same pleasurable feelings. Also, you can easily become addicted, with your body craving stimulation whenever you are not high.

If you are a Christian, the Spirit of God lives within you. Your body is His temple. If you willfully defile your body, God removes His protection from you and allows you to suffer the consequences of your actions. God destroys you by allowing you to destroy yourself. In addition, full recovery isn't guaranteed, even if you stop.

Your body is meant to be holy and dedicated to God, so don't vandalize it.

Adultery

We all know the technical definition of adultery, but Jesus pointed out that it's not quite that simple. The oldest meanings of the word were "to spoil, to break, to destroy." So anytime we let something break our marriage vows, destroy our relationship with our spouse, or spoil the intimacy we share, we have opened the door to adultery. Jesus said that even something as seemingly harmless as ogling someone other than our partner could damage our marriage! God asks us to protect married love, to set a shelter around it that keeps out anything that could threaten it.

Then David said to Nathan, "I have sinned against the Lord."
And Nathan said to him, "The Lord has taken away your sin."

2 SAMUEL 12:13 NLV

" 'For this reason a man will leave his father and mother
and be united to his wife, and the two will become one
flesh.' So they are no longer two, but one flesh. Therefore
what God has joined together, let no one separate."

MATTHEW 19:5–6 NIV

Now a Levite who lived in a remote area in the hill country
of Ephraim took a concubine from Bethlehem in Judah. But
she was unfaithful to him. . . . After she had been [gone] four
months, her husband went to her to persuade her to return.

JUDGES 19:1–3 NIV

No temptation has overtaken you that is not common to
man. God is faithful, and he will not let you be tempted
beyond your ability, but with the temptation he will also
provide the way of escape, that you may be able to endure it.

1 CORINTHIANS 10:13 ESV

Have mercy on me, O God, according to your
steadfast love; according to your abundant mercy
blot out my transgressions. Wash me thoroughly
from my iniquity, and cleanse me from my sin!

PSALM 51:1–2 ESV

After a while his master's wife took notice of Joseph and said, "Come to bed with me!" But he refused. . . . And though she spoke to Joseph day after day, he refused to go to bed with her or even be with her.

GENESIS 39:7–8, 10 NIV

Return to the Lord your God, O Israel, for you have fallen because of your sin. Take words with you and return to the Lord. Say to Him, "Take away all sin, and receive us in kindness, that we may praise You with our lips."

HOSEA 14:1–2 NLV

The teachers of the law and the Pharisees brought in a woman caught in adultery. . . . [Jesus] said to them, "Let any one of you who is without sin be the first to throw a stone at her." . . . Jesus straightened up and asked her, "Woman, where are they? Has no one condemned you?" "No one, sir," she said. "Then neither do I condemn you," Jesus declared. "Go now and leave your life of sin."

JOHN 8:3, 7, 10–11 NIV

You understand us, Lord. You know what we are facing. You have a plan for us. Your Spirit longs to lead us forward into a future of hope and love and strength. We trust in You.

ADULTERY IS DESTRUCTIVE

Adultery is a brainless act,
soul-destroying, self-destructive.
PROVERBS 6:32 MSG

Adultery truly is a mindless act. It is not that adulterers have no brain; the problem is that they are not listening to it. Against their better judgment, in the face of all they know to be true and right, they ignore their rational minds and allow their bodies to be swept along in a tidal wave of lust. Perhaps this tragedy has happened to you—or to your spouse.

God designed the love hormones, dopamine and norepinephrine, to create intense feelings of excitement and romantic passion. He intended a husband and wife to enjoy the pleasures of sex to the full. But He doesn't sanction sex outside of marriage. His Word tells us, "Marriage is honorable among all, and the bed undefiled; but fornicators and adulterers God will judge" (Hebrews 13:4 NKJV).

Now, God will one day judge adulterers, but in the meantime, "a man who commits adultery. . .destroys himself" (Proverbs 6:32 NIV). He destroys integrity, love, trust, his marriage, and sometimes his entire life. If you have gone astray in this way, turn to God, and He will have mercy on you.

ADULTERY IN THE HEART

"Anyone who looks at a woman lustfully has already committed adultery with her in his heart."
MATTHEW 5:28 NIV

Some of Jesus' listeners were astonished when He informed them that a man who looks at a woman with sexual lust and fantasizes about having sex with her has already committed adultery with her in his heart. But that is precisely what he is doing. Jesus didn't say the man had literally committed adultery. He said the man had done it "in his heart."

The Lord also wasn't talking about a passing thought—something most people experience—which they immediately resist. Some people have been needlessly condemned over this. Jesus was talking about focusing on someone with intense desire.

Most people, when they fantasize about having an adulterous affair, purposefully fill their thoughts with lurid mental images. This is what Moses was warning against when he wrote, "You shall not covet your neighbor's wife" (Deuteronomy 5:21 NIV). To "covet" means to earnestly, persistently desire, to set one's heart on something.

Eventually this leads to thoughts of how to actually *have* that person, not merely imagine it. That is why it is vital to not even start down that path.

OBSESSED WITH ADULTERY

*They're obsessed with adultery, compulsive in sin,
seducing every vulnerable soul they come upon.*

2 PETER 2:14 MSG

Many men and women are addicted to adultery. It gives them a rush. They are constantly on the lookout for dissatisfied married people who can be flattered and enticed to indulge in an illicit affair. Many men "creep into households and make captives of gullible women loaded down with sins, led away by various lusts" (2 Timothy 3:6 NKJV).

Of course, some women are the initiators. Like Potiphar's wife, they are continuously looking for new bed partners (Genesis 39:7–12). The Bible warns, "Don't. . .be taken in by her bedroom eyes" (Proverbs 6:25 MSG). And though "the lips of the adulterous woman drip honey" (Proverbs 5:3 NIV), they lead to death.

God knows that even though you are married, you will still find other members of the opposite sex attractive, and at times your hormones will fill you with powerful waves of desire. But don't give in to them, or the day will come when you deeply regret it. Once you have betrayed your husband or wife, it can take a long time and many prayers and tears to rebuild his or her trust.

COMMON SENSE COMMANDMENT

You must not commit adultery.

EXODUS 20:14 NLT

Five short words, but they serve to safeguard you from a very destructive sin. God knew that most people would—at some point or another—be tempted to commit adultery, so He put up a billboard commanding you not to do it.

Remember, "no temptation has overtaken you except what is *common* to mankind" (1 Corinthians 10:13 NIV, emphasis added).

Sexual attraction is a powerful force, and God designed it to help bond husbands and wives together. But even believers, if they are not careful, can be overcome by the siren call of extramarital sex. That is why you must internalize God's command and take steps to keep yourself safe.

You can't keep from noticing that someone is sexually attractive—especially if they have gone to pains to make themselves look that way—but you can keep your eyes from sneaking back for a second and third glance.

If you find your imagination constantly excited by someone else's husband or wife, persistently resist such thoughts. Take definite steps to make sure that you don't ever end up alone with that person. Do this and God will keep you from falling.

HEATING UP OVENS

*"They are all adulterers. Like an oven heated by
a baker. . . . They are all hot, like an oven."*

HOSEA 7:4, 7 NKJV

Feelings of sexual desire can be very powerful. Such passion
is entirely appropriate with your husband or wife but inappropriate outside marriage.

Hosea compared the adulterers of Israel to "an oven heated
by a baker," where the baker added fuel to the barely burning
coals in the oven. Hosea 7:4 (NKJV) adds, "He ceases stirring
the fire after kneading the dough." But up until that time
the baker had worked to *stir up* a blazing fire.

Just so, people who commit adultery usually feed the
flames of desire with sexual images. Adultery is often a
deliberate, premeditated act. One good way to avoid this is
to get rid of any fuel so you can't feed the fire. This means
ridding your home of pornography and refusing to view it
on the Internet. Doing these things will greatly reduce the
problem.

In addition, remember the Bible's advice: "It is better
to marry than to burn with passion" (1 Corinthians 7:9
NKJV). And if you are already married, be satisfied with that
(Proverbs 5:18–20).

Alcohol Abuse

When we abuse alcohol, our relationships suffer. Our physical health suffers. We have less energy for the people and activities we care about most. And most of all, our relationship with God suffers.

God wants us at our best, emotionally, physically, intellectually, socially. Alcohol abuse gets in the way of this. It's not that God is a goody-goody teetotaler! But our deepest connections with Him can thrive only when we are becoming the people He created us to be. He doesn't want anything to hinder that—including alcohol.

But the fruit that comes from having the Holy Spirit in our lives is. . .being the boss over our own desires. . . . If the Holy Spirit is living in us, let us be led by Him in all things.

GALATIANS 5:22–23, 25 NLV

Do not get drunk on wine, which leads to debauchery. Instead, be filled with the Spirit.

EPHESIANS 5:18 NIV

Happy are you, O land, when your king is the son of the nobility, and your princes feast at the proper time, for strength, and not for drunkenness!

ECCLESIASTES 10:17 ESV

"Be careful, or your hearts will be weighed down with carousing, drunkenness and the anxieties of life, and that day will close on you suddenly like a trap."

LUKE 21:34 NIV

Therefore, with minds that are alert and fully sober, set your hope on the grace to be brought to you when Jesus Christ is revealed at his coming.

1 PETER 1:13 NIV

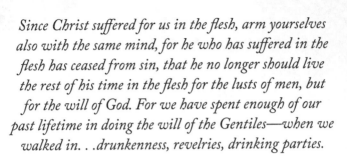

Since Christ suffered for us in the flesh, arm yourselves also with the same mind, for he who has suffered in the flesh has ceased from sin, that he no longer should live the rest of his time in the flesh for the lusts of men, but for the will of God. For we have spent enough of our past lifetime in doing the will of the Gentiles—when we walked in. . .drunkenness, revelries, drinking parties.
1 PETER 4:1–3 NKJV

Wake up from your drunken stupor, as is right, and do not go on sinning.
1 CORINTHIANS 15:34 ESV

No temptation has overtaken you except such as is common to man; but God is faithful, who will not allow you to be tempted beyond what you are able, but with the temptation will also make the way of escape, that you may be able to bear it.
1 CORINTHIANS 10:13 NKJV

I know You are helping me, Jesus. I believe You are with me. Please send human helpers too. Give me the courage to let others know I have this problem—and then to ask for their help. Help me to focus outward, on others, rather than on my own situation. Give me a strong network to depend on so that I can learn new ways to live.

OVERCOMING ALCOHOLISM

Who has needless bruises? Who has bloodshot
eyes? Those who linger over wine.
PROVERBS 23:29–30 NIV

If you have a problem with alcohol, you don't need to be told that it is wrong. You already know that. You know that it is wasting your hard-earned cash, that it is wrecking your marriage, and that it leaves you filled with remorse and despair. And then there are those totally needless bruises. The question is, what are you going to do about it?

Until you are desperate enough to surrender your life to God, there is not a whole lot you can do. You have already tried to stop yourself but have repeatedly fallen off the wagon.

Here is where the biblical principles behind Alcoholics Anonymous can help: you must honestly admit your sins, confess your faults to someone else, and trust God for the power to change. There is more to it, but these are an excellent start.

As a Christian, you know that the Higher Power is Jesus, the Son of God. He said, "Apart from me you can do nothing" (John 15:5 NIV). And Paul wrote, "I can do everything through Christ, who gives me strength" (Philippians 4:13 NLT).

DOWNSIDES OF ALCOHOL

Wine produces mockers; alcohol leads to brawls.
Those led astray by drink cannot be wise.

PROVERBS 20:1 NLT

Alcohol removes inhibitions and sets people's base natures loose. A person under the influence of drink is often loud and confrontational. Some people become happy and make jokes or boast; others become angry and mock or argue. The latter often leads to drunken fights.

"Those led astray by drink cannot be wise." Have you ever seen an inebriated man giving someone advice? Though he may think he is sharing words of profound wisdom, to the sober listener it is utter foolishness.

The only time you can be truly wise is when you are sober. That is when it pays to take a long, hard look at the benefits and downsides of drinking. Alcohol does offer a temporary escape from trouble. This is why many people turn to it to unwind and forget or to have a "good time." Unfortunately, it also causes many problems, problems that are not temporary.

If you struggle with alcohol, it is wise to make yourself accountable to others who understand your struggle. Listen to their advice and then act on it day by day.

BOASTING ABOUT DRINKING

What sorrow for those who are heroes at drinking
wine and boast about all the alcohol they can hold.

ISAIAH 5:22 NLT

Sometimes what you thought was a strength, something to be proud of, was actually a weakness. The fact that you once boasted about your drinking was a sure sign that you had set yourself up for grief. If you now have sobriety, you can look back and shake your head in disbelief at such a mindset.

If you are still struggling to gain mastery over the bottle, you may already be aware that boasting about how much liquor you can hold is stupid. But knowing that isn't enough. You can still be fooled by thinking, "But one drink can't hurt, since, after all, it takes a lot for me to get drunk." But one glass leads to many more.

If you have any pride left at all about drinking, or if you are still amused by your antics when intoxicated, you are not ready to abandon alcohol and put your life back together. As cliché as this sounds, you actually have to hit rock bottom before you are ready for God's solution.

GETTING FLAMING DRUNK

What sorrow for those who. . . spend long evenings drinking wine to make themselves flaming drunk.

ISAIAH 5:11 NLT

Those who have a full-blown case of alcoholism have little control over their addiction. However, not all people have an advanced case of this addiction, particularly at the beginning. Often, when they are first giving in to drink, they have a choice in the matter.

That is why the Bible warns you not to binge drink just to experience what it is like to be completely drunk. Not only are you starting down a very slippery slope that could become a lifelong habit of destruction, but think of the damage you can cause in just one night!

The young are especially tempted to prove how much alcohol they can hold or just how much of a spectacle they are willing to make of themselves. Many see out-of-control drunkenness as a rite of passage or a way to earn respect or acceptance. What sorrow they earn instead!

Why wait until things get so bad that alcohol has become your master and you must fight a protracted battle to take back your life? It is better to stop before you even start.

Anger

The Bible tells us not to nurse our anger. Instead of dwelling on it, the psalmist says we should turn away from it. Instead of feeding it until we explode, we are to let it go. There's nothing wrong with feeling angry sometimes—but when we let our anger drive us, when we lose control of ourselves because we're so full of rage, then we're likely to hurt those around us.

Acknowledge your angry feelings. But then give them to God. Allow Him to be the container that holds your temper—and keeps it from hurting others.

Stop being angry. Turn away from fighting.
Do not trouble yourself. It leads only to wrong-doing.
PSALM 37:8 NLV

Do not make friends with a hot-tempered person,
do not associate with one easily angered.
PROVERBS 22:24 NIV

Men who speak against others set a city
on fire, but wise men turn away anger.
PROVERBS 29:8 NLV

If you are angry, do not let it become sin.
Get over your anger before the day is finished.
EPHESIANS 4:26 NLV

A hot-tempered person stirs up conflict, but
the one who is patient calms a quarrel.
PROVERBS 15:18 NIV

Whoever is slow to anger is better than the mighty,
and he who rules his spirit than he who takes a city.
PROVERBS 16:32 ESV

Good sense makes one slow to anger,
and it is his glory to overlook an offense.
PROVERBS 19:11 ESV

Wherefore, my beloved brethren, let every man
be swift to hear, slow to speak, slow to wrath.
JAMES 1:19 KJV

A hot-tempered person must pay the penalty;
rescue them, and you will have to do it again.
PROVERBS 19:19 NIV

Like a city whose walls are broken through
is a person who lacks self-control.
PROVERBS 25:28 NIV

The vexation of a fool is known at once,
but the prudent ignores an insult.
PROVERBS 12:16 ESV

Fathers, do not provoke your children,
lest they become discouraged.
COLOSSIANS 3:21 NKJV

A stone is heavy, and the sand weighty; but a fool's wrath
is heavier than them both. Wrath is cruel, and anger is
outrageous; but who is able to stand before envy?
PROVERBS 27:3–4 KJV

Put out of your life all these things: bad feelings about
other people, anger, temper, loud talk, bad talk which hurts
other people, and bad feelings which hurt other people.
EPHESIANS 4:31 NLV

The proud and arrogant person—"Mocker"
is his name—behaves with insolent fury.
PROVERBS 21:24 NIV

A gentle answer turns away wrath,
but a harsh word stirs up anger.
PROVERBS 15:1 NIV

If the ruler becomes angry with you, do not back away.
If you are quiet, much wrong-doing may be put aside.
ECCLESIASTES 10:4 NLV

I desire therefore that the men pray everywhere,
lifting up holy hands, without wrath and doubting.
1 TIMOTHY 2:8 NKJV

God, remind me that the sun should not go down on
my anger. Help me not to go to bed nursing a grudge
that will haunt my sleep and get up with me in the
morning. Instead, let me value my relationships enough
that I commit myself to working through the conflicts
that arise. I know You want us to live in harmony.

CONTROLLING YOUR TEMPER

Do not hasten in your spirit to be angry,
for anger rests in the bosom of fools.
ECCLESIASTES 7:9 NKJV

The New International Version says it this way: "Do not be quickly provoked in your spirit." In other words, exercise self-control and don't allow yourself to be easily provoked. Whether you believe that you can do it or not, God expects you to be able to control your temper.

James writes, "Let every man be. . .slow to wrath" (James 1:19 NKJV), and you might have to bite down on your tongue to avoid giving in to it.

The Bible also says, "A fool's wrath is known at once. . . . A fool rages. . . . A quick-tempered man acts foolishly" (Proverbs 12:16; 14:16, 17 NKJV). Remind yourself: if you continue to lose your temper easily, you are behaving like a fool—and the Bible gives clear warnings about fools: "The mouth of the foolish is near destruction. . . . A fool lays open his folly. . . . The foolishness of a man twists his way. . . . A fool vents all his feelings" (Proverbs 10:14; 13:16; 19:3; 29:11 NKJV). Exercising self-control is well worth it.

BE SLOW TO ANGER

Let every man be swift to hear,
slow to speak, slow to wrath.
JAMES 1:19 KJV

Many people are easygoing. They don't rile easily. Other people have a short fuse and struggle with anger issues most of their lives. They know they should simply let things go, but at the slightest provocation, their temper flares up. Is there no solution?

There may not be an easy solution, but there is a solution. James tells us, "Let every man be. . .slow to wrath" (James 1:19 KJV). He says "*every* man" (emphasis added). This tells us that with God's help, we all can gain control of our tempers. No exceptions.

However, we often first need to renounce our pride. Some people actually boast, "Whoa! You should see me when I get mad!" The Bible addresses pride-motivated statements, saying, "All such boasting is evil" (James 4:16 NKJV).

Second, we must cry out to God for help. Third, we need to make a constant effort to have patience. If we give others the benefit of the doubt and don't jump to conclusions, we can defuse many arguments and provocations before they begin.

HOT TEMPERS AND CONFLICT

An angry person stirs up conflict, and a
hot-tempered person commits many sins.

PROVERBS 29:22 NIV

Whether you are an angry person or are close to an angry person, you know how easily someone with a temper can be set off. At the slightest provocation, voices are raised, accusations are made, and the fight is on. Lighting an angry person's fuse is easy, and once lit, the person explodes.

Pride and a brooding sense of injustice are often at the root. Angry people are quick to imagine that someone has insulted them and to take offense. They constantly stir up fights and in the process commit many sins.

Try this: *pray* for those who anger you, commit them into God's hands, ask Him to bless them richly, and pray that He will give you love, empathy, and understanding for them. "The LORD turned the captivity of Job, when he prayed for his friends" (Job 42:10 KJV).

When you earnestly pray for others' good, you more easily forgive and overlook their faults. And if you are overlooking their faults, you won't be prone to be angry with them.

QUICK-TEMPERED FOLLY

Whoever is patient has great understanding,
but one who is quick-tempered displays folly.

PROVERBS 14:29 NIV

If you are plagued by a quick temper, it might seem frustrating to hear that the solution is to have lots of patience—as if there were a choice in the matter! Your anger might appear to be like a tidal wave that rises up in an instant without warning, at the slightest provocation. It might seem as if you have no control over it.

The truth is, however, that you can eventually master it if you are determined to do so. It will take time and concentrated effort, and it may even take attending a few anger management courses. But the more you understand why you react the way you do and recognize your trigger points, the more control you will have.

Another strategy for reining in your temper is to make a concerted effort to understand others as well. If you begin to understand what motivates them, you are less likely to take offense. And if you determine to be patient with people and to love them with God's love, you can actually begin to govern your anger.

ANGER MANAGEMENT

Sensible people control their temper;
they earn respect by overlooking wrongs.
PROVERBS 19:11 NLT

Even smart people can have a quick temper. However, they recognize that their anger is a problem, so they take steps to control it. They don't want to hurt others or make a bad situation worse.

If you have anger issues, there are things you can do. First, the Bible says to overlook wrongs. Solomon said, "Do not pay attention to every word people say" (Ecclesiastes 7:21 NIV), but remind yourself that you too say things you shouldn't (v. 22). If you can, let it pass.

Second, make up your mind ahead of time that, when provoked, you won't respond with an angry outburst.

Third, don't answer quickly, but take time to pray and think through a calm response.

Fourth, when you express yourself, avoid making blanket accusations such as, "You always. . ." Instead, explain how the offender's actions or words make you feel.

Fifth, instead of focusing on what made you angry, suggest solutions to the problem.

Sixth, when really angry, take some time out to exercise.

Seventh, pray and meditate on peaceful subjects before reengaging with the person who offended you.

Anxiety

It's easy to be anxious. Are our loved ones safe? Will we have enough money for what we need? Will our friends accept us? Will we be able to get everything done? Anxieties pile up around us everywhere we turn.

We need to learn to transform our anxiety into prayer. Each time we find ourselves fretting over what will happen regarding some situation, we can turn over that specific set of circumstances to God. As we make this practice a habit, we will find our trust in God growing. Instead of anxiety, Christ will dwell at the center of our lives.

Cast all your anxiety on him because he cares for you.
1 PETER 5:7 NIV

Trust in the LORD with all thine heart; and lean not unto thine own understanding. In all thy ways acknowledge him, and he shall direct thy paths.
PROVERBS 3:5–6 KJV

Be anxious for nothing, but in everything by prayer and supplication, with thanksgiving, let your requests be made known to God; and the peace of God, which surpasses all understanding, will guard your hearts and minds through Christ Jesus.
PHILIPPIANS 4:6–7 NKJV

Anxiety weighs down the heart, but a kind word cheers it up.
PROVERBS 12:25 NIV

My people will abide in a peaceful habitation, in secure dwellings, and in quiet resting places.
ISAIAH 32:18 ESV

Some trust in chariots and some in horses, but we trust in the name of the LORD our God.
PSALM 20:7 NIV

"The seed that was planted among thorns is like some people who listen to the Word. But the cares of this life let thorns come up. A love for riches and always wanting other things let thorns grow. These things do not give the Word room to grow so it does not give grain."

MARK 4:18–19 NLV

When anxiety was great within me, your consolation brought me joy.

PSALM 94:19 NIV

The Lord says, "Stand by where the roads cross, and look. Ask for the old paths, where the good way is, and walk in it. And you will find rest for your souls.

JEREMIAH 6:16 NLV

Surely I have calmed and quieted my soul, like a weaned child with his mother; like a weaned child is my soul within me.

PSALM 131:2 NKJV

Trust in the LORD and do good; dwell in the land and enjoy safe pasture.

PSALM 37:3 NIV

These things I have spoken unto you, that in me ye might have peace. In the world ye shall have tribulation: but be of good cheer; I have overcome the world.

JOHN 16:33 KJV

But godliness with contentment is great gain.
1 TIMOTHY 6:6 KJV

Unless the Lord builds the house, its builders work for nothing. Unless the Lord watches over the city, the men who watch over it stay awake for nothing. You rise up early, and go to bed late, and work hard for your food, all for nothing. For the Lord gives to His loved ones even while they sleep.
PSALM 127:1–2 NLV

Trouble and anguish have found me out, but your commandments are my delight.
PSALM 119:143 ESV

First of all, look for the holy nation of God. Be right with Him. All these other things will be given to you also.
MATTHEW 6:33 NLV

Indeed, he who watches over Israel will neither slumber nor sleep.
PSALM 121:4 NIV

For in Scripture it says: "See, I lay a stone in Zion, a chosen and precious cornerstone, and the one who trusts in him will never be put to shame." Now to you who believe, this stone is precious. But to those who do not believe, "The stone the builders rejected has become the cornerstone."
1 PETER 2:6–7 NIV

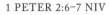

*Better is a handful of quietness than two hands
full of toil and a striving after wind.*

ECCLESIASTES 4:6 ESV

*The Lord is my strength and my safe cover. My
heart trusts in Him, and I am helped. So my heart
is full of joy. I will thank Him with my song.*

PSALM 28:7 NLV

*Wait for the L*ORD*; be strong, and let your
heart take courage; wait for the L*ORD*!*

PSALM 27:14 ESV

*"The L*ORD *turn his face toward you and give you peace."*

NUMBERS 6:26 NIV

*Then they were glad that the waters were quiet,
and he brought them to their desired haven.*

PSALM 107:30 ESV

---

*When everything is going well, I'm not too anxious, Lord.
I feel like I'm in control. My sense of security is stable.
But when I feel threatened or overwhelmed, I start to
get anxious. Use my anxiety, Lord, to remind me that
I'm dependent on Your love. Let each nagging fear be a
nudge that turns me toward You and Your strength.*

AVOIDING ANXIETY

So what do people get. . .for all their hard work
and anxiety?. . . At night their minds cannot rest.
ECCLESIASTES 2:22–23 NLT

A habit of worry leads to an anxious mind. Anxiety is a decision to not trust God and instead scramble around trying to solve your own problems. You may find yourself slipping so naturally into a worried attitude that it doesn't even seem like a conscious decision. But it is.

What starts off as a small worry quickly grows into a frenzied effort to work things out. But it is all a waste of time.

The first step to overcoming anxiety is to realize that worrying is a surefire way to sabotage success. Being anxious all day is very tiring, yet it robs you of sleep at night. And knowing that you won't be able to do your best if you are sleep deprived gives you something else to worry about.

The best way to fight anxiety is to continually look to the Lord, constantly quote Bible promises to yourself, and refuse to give an inch to worry. It will be hard at first but don't worry: it gets easier as time goes on.

WEARING YOURSELF OUT

It is useless for you to work so hard from early morning until late at night, anxiously working for food to eat; for God gives rest to his loved ones.

PSALM 127:2 NLT

Many people think that worry is a trifling thing, something that frays the outer edges of their minds but really isn't a problem. But anxiety can suck the very life out of you. If you fear that setbacks are inevitable and constantly fret that your finances aren't sufficient, you will work harder to compensate for the lack. And if you work when you should be resting, you will wear yourself out.

The thing is, there may not even be a lack on your horizon. You just worry that there will be. So you give yourself stomach ulcers and overwork for nothing. Now, it is prudent to make sure that you have sufficient finances, but anxiety is beyond prudent. It's a failure to believe that God cares for you.

David wrote, "In the multitude of my anxieties within me, Your comforts delight my soul" (Psalm 94:19 NKJV). David did what he could, but after that he trusted the Lord and allowed God to comfort him.

DON'T BE ANXIOUS

Do not be anxious about anything, but in every
situation. . .present your requests to God.
PHILIPPIANS 4:6 NIV

Say you are out shopping and you suddenly realize you have lost your keys or your iPhone. You are hit with panic, and as time crawls on, you get a sinking feeling of how bad this situation is. The normal tendency is to let wave after wave of anxiety roll over you.

But the Bible says, "Do not be anxious about *anything*, but in *every* situation. . .present your requests to God" (Philippians 4:6 NIV, emphasis added). No exceptions. So that is what you should do: ask God to do a miracle and help you locate it or have some honest person find it and turn it in.

It doesn't have to be an emergency either. It could simply be a situation that is bad and slowly getting worse, and over which you have little control. Rather than letting it suck the life out of you, you need to be able to turn it over to God.

You aren't guaranteed that God will reunite you with your missing items, but He can at least limit the damage that their loss may cause.

Arguments

God doesn't want us to quarrel. He calls us instead to kindness. This may mean setting our own opinions aside as being not all that important. . .so that instead we can hear what another thinks. It may mean letting go of our own choices. . .so we can make room for another to choose. It may require that we keep our mouth shut when angry words threaten to burst out of us. . .so that someone else has a chance to speak.

Does it (whatever "it" is) really matter that much? Or can we choose to make kindness matter far more?

What causes fights and quarrels among you? Don't they come from your desires that battle within you? You desire but do not have, so you kill. You covet but you cannot get what you want, so you quarrel and fight. . . . You adulterous people, don't you know that friendship with the world means enmity against God? . . . But he gives us more grace. That is why Scripture says: "God opposes the proud but shows favor to the humble." Submit yourselves, then, to God. Resist the devil, and he will flee from you. Come near to God and he will come near to you. Wash your hands, you sinners, and purify your hearts, you double-minded. . . . Humble yourselves before the Lord, and he will lift you up.

JAMES 4:1–2, 4, 6–8, 10 NIV

Don't have anything to do with foolish and stupid arguments, because you know they produce quarrels. And the Lord's servant must not be quarrelsome but must be kind to everyone, able to teach, not resentful.

2 TIMOTHY 2:23–24 NIV

I want you to stress these things, so that those who have trusted in God may be careful to devote themselves to doing what is good. These things are excellent and profitable for everyone. But avoid foolish controversies and genealogies and arguments and quarrels about the law, because these are unprofitable and useless. Warn a divisive person once, and then warn them a second time. After that, have nothing to do with them.

TITUS 3:8–10 NIV

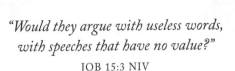

"Would they argue with useless words,
with speeches that have no value?"

JOB 15:3 NIV

No one wants what is right and fair in court. And no one
argues his cause with the truth. They trust in what is false, and
speak lies. They plan to make trouble and do what is sinful.

ISAIAH 59:4 NLV

Put on therefore, as the elect of God, holy and beloved,
bowels of mercies, kindness, humbleness of mind,
meekness, longsuffering; forbearing one another, and
forgiving one another, if any man have a quarrel
against any: even as Christ forgave you, so also do ye.

COLOSSIANS 3:12 –13 KJV

An argument started among the disciples as to which of them
would be the greatest. Jesus, knowing their thoughts, took a
little child and had him stand beside him. Then he said to them,
"Whoever welcomes this little child in my name welcomes me;
and whoever welcomes me welcomes the one who sent me. For
it is the one who is least among you all who is the greatest."

LUKE 9:46–48 NIV

We demolish arguments and every pretension that sets
itself up against the knowledge of God, and we take
captive every thought to make it obedient to Christ.

2 CORINTHIANS 10:5 NIV

Do all things without grumbling or disputing, that you may be blameless and innocent, children of God without blemish in the midst of a crooked and twisted generation, among whom you shine as lights in the world, holding fast to the word of life, so that in the day of Christ I may be proud that I did not run in vain or labor in vain.

PHILIPPIANS 2:14–16 ESV

I tell you this so that no one may deceive you by fine-sounding arguments. For though I am absent from you in body, I am present with you in spirit and delight to see how disciplined you are and how firm your faith in Christ is.

COLOSSIANS 2:4–5 NIV

May I use my conversations only for Your glory, Lord. Remind me to seek to bless others with each thing I say. If arguments and cross words pour out of me, how can I claim to be filled with Your Spirit? Cleanse my heart first, dear God, and then my mouth and all its words, so that my life is not filled with contradiction.

PRIDE AND ARGUING

By pride comes nothing but strife.
PROVERBS 13:10 NKJV

You may like to think that you are reasonable and that when you disagree with someone you base your arguments only on facts. But most people are motivated by a number of factors—pride being chief among them.

Try this: Watch others argue and listen to their reasoning and logic. But also observe their facial expressions and body language, and pay attention to the tone of their voices. Do voices become raised and faces angry and flushed when debating? This is proof that strong emotions are involved. Do they resort to mockery to negate sound reasoning? Do they use humor, sarcasm, or zingers to try to score major points?

Let's face it: many arguments are caused by nothing but pride. Someone feels threatened and so refuses to acknowledge that the other person is right at all. Or she has been offended and so bristles up and quarrels. Or he feels mistreated and so argues out of a sense of injustice—barely even listening to what the other person is saying.

We all have been guilty of these things, so let's walk in a spirit of humility and disagree politely.

SENSELESS QUARRELS

Don't have anything to do with foolish and stupid
arguments, because you know they produce quarrels.
2 TIMOTHY 2:23 NIV

If you happen to walk by two neighbors arguing, and one of them is making ridiculous or irrational claims, you may be tempted to stop and try to set that person straight. Don't. It's very often not worth the trouble.

"Interfering in someone else's argument is as foolish as yanking a dog's ears" (Proverbs 26:17 NLT). What happens when you do that? The dog bites you, of course. For the same reason, Jesus said, "Don't throw your pearls to pigs! They will trample the pearls, then turn and attack you" (Matthew 7:6 NLT).

When people are making pigheaded arguments, they are not open to reason. And many people argue from an emotional basis, which is why they are not convinced by even the most rational explanations.

Don't even answer those seeking to drag you into a quarrel. If they are looking for a fight, there is no way you can win. You will just end up raving like them. "Don't answer the foolish arguments of fools, or you will become as foolish as they are" (Proverbs 26:4 NLT).

AVOID ARGUMENTATIVE PEOPLE

Stay away from mindless, pointless quarreling.
TITUS 3:9 MSG

There is no way to have a rational discussion with a person who loves to argue. Any disagreement quickly descends into pointless quarreling. They either end up yelling at you or mocking you. "If a wise man contends with a foolish man, whether the fool rages or laughs, there is no peace" (Proverbs 29:9 NKJV).

Do your best to avoid argumentative people. If you can't avoid them, resolutely refuse to be drawn into quarrels with them. It is simply not worth the trouble. And if it means letting them think they got the better of you, let them think that.

This doesn't mean you can't have any relationship with such people. You may have to maintain a rapport with them if they are family members or workmates.

Paul instructed church leaders, "Warn a quarrelsome person once or twice, but then be done with him" (Titus 3:10 MSG). When it becomes obvious that someone is fully set in their ways, you need to have the wisdom to refrain from trying to convince them or change them. Instead, pray for them.

AVOIDING QUARRELS

Starting a quarrel is like breaching a dam;
so drop the matter before a dispute breaks out.
PROVERBS 17:14 NIV

They didn't have huge hydroelectric dams in Bible days. The dams that existed were usually pond-sized irrigation reservoirs, and the water was held back by walls of hard-packed dirt. One farmer with a pickax could easily breach it. And once the water started to rush out and sweep away more and more of the restraining wall, there was no way to stop it.

Sometimes when you tell a friend you are going to confront somebody, they ask, "Is this the hill you want to die on?" In other words, given its potential for causing unwanted trouble and repercussions, is the confrontation really worth engaging in?

Some issues are well worth disputing, make no mistake about it. But disputing out of pride or to put somebody "in his place," simply isn't worth it. And the problem is, once you start the process, you have stirred up the other person, and the war is on.

How do you know when to contend and when to drop a matter? "A wise man's heart discerns both time and judgment" (Ecclesiastes 8:5 NKJV).

KEEP YOUR COOL

*A servant of the Lord must not quarrel but must be kind
to everyone. . .and be patient with difficult people.*
2 TIMOTHY 2:24 NLT

You may think, *"Be kind to everyone"? Sure, I can manage that.*
But you stop short at the next part: "Be patient with difficult
people." You think, *I don't take grief from anybody. If someone
is ornery, I'll tell them off.* So much for being kind to *everyone.*

When scripture says you "must not quarrel," it means
exactly that. You must not quarrel even with cantankerous
individuals. And how do you avoid it? By being kind to
everyone.

There is a difference between quarrels and disagreements.
Sometimes we have no choice but to dispute with someone,
whether the person is ornery or not. But the main reason we
are advised not to quarrel with difficult persons is that we
won't get anywhere by doing so. We will just waste our time.

Some people love a good argument. For them, it is important to win a debate, but it is more important to get the
satisfaction of yelling at the other person and putting that
person in his or her place. But that is not God's way of doing
things.

Betrayal

People let us down. Sometimes it's unintentional, and that hurts bad enough. It's even worse when a friend purposely stabs us in the back. The hurt can be overwhelming. It's only natural to want to put up our guard.

It's far more challenging to follow Christ's example. He too knew what it was like to be betrayed by a friend. And yet He never spoke sharp words, never sought to return the blow in any way.

If we are followers of Jesus Christ, then we too must find ways to respond with love to those who have hurt us.

And while they abode in Galilee, Jesus said unto them, The Son of man shall be betrayed into the hands of men: and they shall kill him, and the third day he shall be raised again.

MATTHEW 17:22–23 KJV

"If his sons forsake my law and do not follow my statutes, if they violate my decrees and fail to keep my commands, I will punish their sin with the rod, their iniquity with flogging; but I will not take my love from him, nor will I ever betray my faithfulness."

PSALM 89:30–33 NIV

There are six things which the Lord hates, yes, seven that are hated by Him. . .a person who tells lies about someone else. . . . My son, keep the teaching of your father, and do not turn away from the teaching of your mother. Hold them always to your heart. Tie them around your neck. They will lead you when you walk. They will watch over you when you sleep, and they will talk with you when you wake up. For the word is a lamp. The teaching is a light.

PROVERBS 6:16, 19–23 NLV

My companion attacks his friends; he violates his covenant. His talk is smooth as butter, yet war is in his heart; his words are more soothing than oil, yet they are drawn swords. Cast your cares on the LORD and he will sustain you; he will never let the righteous be shaken.

PSALM 55:20–22 NIV

For I have received of the Lord that which also I delivered unto you, that the Lord Jesus the same night in which he was betrayed took bread: and when he had given thanks, he brake it, and said, Take, eat: this is my body, which is broken for you: this do in remembrance of me.

1 CORINTHIANS 11:23–24 KJV

Preserve me, O God, for in you I take refuge. I say to the LORD, "You are my Lord; I have no good apart from you.". . . Therefore my heart is glad, and my whole being rejoices; my flesh also dwells secure. For you will not abandon my soul.

PSALM 16:1–2, 9–10 ESV

And David went out to meet them, and answered and said unto them, If ye be come peaceably unto me to help me, mine heart shall be knit unto you: but if ye be come to betray me to mine enemies, seeing there is no wrong in mine hands, the God of our fathers look thereon, and rebuke it.

1 CHRONICLES 12:17 KJV

See that no one repays anyone evil for evil, but always seek to do good to one another and to everyone. Rejoice always, pray without ceasing, give thanks in all circumstances; for this is the will of God in Christ Jesus for you.

1 THESSALONIANS 5:15–18 ESV

The eyes of the LORD keep watch over knowledge, but he overthrows the words of the traitor.

PROVERBS 22:12 ESV

"You will be betrayed even by parents, brothers and sisters, relatives and friends, and they will put some of you to death. Everyone will hate you because of me. But not a hair of your head will perish. Stand firm, and you will win life."

LUKE 21:16–19 NIV

*Know therefore that the L*ORD *your God is God, the faithful God who keeps covenant and steadfast love with those who love him and keep his commandments, to a thousand generations.*

DEUTERONOMY 7:9 ESV

*Ah, you destroyer, who yourself have not been destroyed, you traitor, whom none has betrayed! When you have ceased to destroy, you will be destroyed; and when you have finished betraying, they will betray you. O L*ORD, *be gracious to us; we wait for you. Be our arm every morning, our salvation in the time of trouble.*

ISAIAH 33:1–2 ESV

Use my pain at this betrayal for Your purposes, Creator God. Teach me through it. Draw me closer to You. Deepen my compassion for others.

WHEN FRIENDS BETRAY YOU

Even my best friend, the one I trusted completely,
the one who shared my food, has turned against me.
PSALM 41:9 NLT

Betrayal hurts, especially when the person who betrayed you was a close friend, someone you shared your most intimate thoughts with. You trusted him. Then you learned that he went about as a gossip, either carelessly or maliciously telling your deepest secrets.

We all have experienced betrayal in one form or another. Perhaps you have betrayed someone. Even if you didn't intentionally cross her, she feels that you did, or that you went back on your word, let her down, or told others things she had confided to you.

It is difficult to make amends if the one you betrayed no longer wishes to speak to you and refuses to trust you again. Since you know how that feels, make sure never to put someone else through the wringer for a similar blunder.

Discern between a malicious betrayal (by someone you must avoid confiding in again) and a friend who made an honest mistake (but who deserves another chance, and whom you can still trust). Forgive everyone, but use wisdom in restoring people to your confidence.

UNTRUSTWORTHY GOSSIPS

A gadabout gossip can't be trusted with a secret.
PROVERBS 11:13 MSG

Sometimes you let down your guard and tell another person confidential things you probably shouldn't. He is your friend. You trust him. What could go wrong? But misunderstandings happen, and when they do, friends get offended. And then a friend, who now has a grudge against you, is in possession of information that could cause you embarrassment or damage.

Or maybe there was no misunderstanding. Maybe a friend simply wasn't trustworthy to begin with, because she just couldn't resist the temptation to share some juicy gossip.

Sometimes you are blindsided by betrayal. But often you set yourself up for pain by trusting someone against your better judgment. This is why David wrote, "I will hold my tongue when the ungodly are around me" (Psalm 39:1 NLT). And at times you need to refrain from telling *anyone*. "Don't trust your neighbor, don't confide in your friend" (Micah 7:5 MSG).

Of course, you need to be able to share your heart with friends, and fortunately there *are* good, trustworthy people. Know who can be trusted and stick to confiding in them.

A LEGACY OF ABUSE

*Those who betray their own friends leave
a legacy of abuse to their children.*

JOB 17:5 MSG

Some people are users. They feel that other people exist for their benefit, perhaps to borrow money from (with no intention of repaying) or to use for momentary sexual gratification, and then to toss aside. They befriend people, intending to use them and betray their trust.

If you have suffered at the hands of such people, learn to recognize them and to avoid being taken in. Learn to say no to their sob stories, and refuse to let them use you again.

"They are like shameless shepherds who care only for themselves. They are like clouds blowing over the land without giving any rain. . . . They are like wild waves of the sea, churning up the foam of their shameful deeds" (Jude 1:12–13 NLT).

While they are hurting others, they are living a self-destructive lifestyle, and they themselves will eventually suffer most. Such lack of concern and loyalty eventually comes back to haunt them, wreaking havoc in their own lives and in the lives of their children, who are influenced by their lack of morals.

RESPONDING TO BETRAYAL

*"Then many will be offended, will betray
one another, and will hate one another."*

MATTHEW 24:10 NKJV

Chances are, someone whom you trusted has ended up betraying you. In a society dominated by self-centered attitudes, it is not surprising to see loyalties and friendships casually cast aside. It is a sign of the times, the steady deterioration of a once-moral society.

Jesus warned that in the last days many people would abandon their faith and would betray their former fellow believers. But how are you supposed to respond in such cases—and how should you react when someone betrays you for any reason?

Jesus gave the answer when He said, "Love your enemies, do good to those who hate you, bless those who curse you, and pray for those who spitefully use you" (Luke 6:27–28 NKJV). Yes, He expects you to forgive someone who has betrayed you, even if you can no longer trust that person and would no longer choose them as a confidant and friend.

It is important for your own sake that you forgive them. That way you keep your life free from bitterness, and you are not carrying hatred around inside you.

Challenges

We're not likely to ever face an army of horses and chariots—but some days, the challenges in our lives can seem just as threatening as any battlefield. When that happens, we need to follow the advice given in the Bible. First, remember all that God has done for us in the past. Second, believe that He is the One who will fight our battles, not us. We can rely on Him for the victory.

The load was so heavy we did not have the strength to keep going. . . . This happened so we would not put our trust in ourselves, but in God Who raises the dead.

2 CORINTHIANS 1:8–9 NLV

I also persevered in the work on this wall, and we acquired no land, and all my servants were gathered there for the work. Moreover, there were at my table 150 men, Jews and officials, besides those who came to us from the nations that were around us. Now what was prepared at my expense for each day was one ox and six choice sheep and birds, and every ten days all kinds of wine in abundance. Yet for all this I did not demand the food allowance of the governor, because the service was too heavy on this people. Remember for my good, O my God, all that I have done for this people.

NEHEMIAH 5:16–19 ESV

"Have I not commanded you? Be strong and courageous. Do not be afraid; do not be discouraged, for the LORD your God will be with you wherever you go."

JOSHUA 1:9 NIV

You need to persevere so that when you have done the will of God, you will receive what he has promised.

HEBREWS 10:36 NIV

"If what is bad comes upon us, fighting, hard times, disease, or no food, we will stand in front of this house. And we will stand before You, (for Your name is in this house). We will cry to You in our trouble. And You will hear and take us out of trouble."

2 CHRONICLES 20:9 NLV

Then the Lord said to Moses, "Why do you cry to me? Tell the people of Israel to keep going. Lift up your special stick and put out your hand over the sea, and divide it. Then the people of Israel will go through the sea on dry land."

EXODUS 14:15–16 NLV

Brothers and sisters, as an example of patience in the face of suffering, take the prophets who spoke in the name of the Lord. As you know, we count as blessed those who have persevered. You have heard of Job's perseverance and have seen what the Lord finally brought about. The Lord is full of compassion and mercy.

JAMES 5:10–11 NIV

*By faith he left Egypt, not fearing the king's anger;
he persevered because he saw him who is invisible.*
HEBREWS 11:27 NIV

*"Many people will give up and turn away at this time.
People will hand over each other. They will hate each other.
Many false religious teachers will come. They will fool
many people and will turn them to the wrong way. Because
of people breaking the laws and sin being everywhere,
the love in the hearts of many people will become cold.
But the one who stays true to the end will be saved."*
MATTHEW 24:10–13 NLV

*"In this world you will have trouble. But take
heart! I have overcome the world."*
JOHN 16:33 NIV

*But Jesus looked at them and said to them, "With men
this is impossible, but with God all things are possible."*
MATTHEW 19:26 NKJV

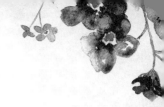

"*Because you have kept My command to persevere,
I also will keep you from the hour of trial which shall
come upon the whole world, to test those who dwell
on the earth. Behold, I am coming quickly! Hold fast
what you have, that no one may take your crown.*"

REVELATION 3:10–11 NKJV

---

*The challenge that lies ahead, Lord, is too big for me. My
self-confidence fails. I can't help but compare the enormity
of the challenge to my meager ability to confront it. My
faith wavers. But I know that when I admit how weak
I truly am, then You have the chance to reveal Your
strength. The challenge that lies ahead shrinks when I
compare it to the immensity of You. And I finally realize
that my perception of the challenge depends on my
perspective. Keep me focused on You and Your power.*

EYES ON GOD

"O our God, will You not judge them?
For we have no power. . .nor do we know
what to do, but our eyes are upon You."

2 CHRONICLES 20:12 NKJV

Christians are no strangers to problems. Sometimes it may seem that your life is *filled* with challenges, setbacks, and obstacles. At such times, you can only look to God and cry out, "Do not withhold Your tender mercies from me, O LORD. . . . For innumerable evils have surrounded me" (Psalm 40:11–12 NKJV).

These challenges could be opposition in the workplace, financial problems, serious long-term illnesses, or malicious people who seek to ruin your reputation.

In King Jehoshaphat's day, three enemy nations invaded Judah. They vastly outnumbered the Jews. Jehoshaphat and his people were overwhelmed. They had no idea what to do because there was nothing they could do. So they looked to God and cried out to Him.

God did a miracle to deliver them. And He can do the same for you today. He promises in His Word, "You will seek me and find me when you seek me with all your heart" (Jeremiah 29:13 NIV).

RELIEF FROM ATTACKS

Be merciful to me, O God, for man would
swallow me up; fighting all day he oppresses me.
PSALM 56:1 NKJV

Sometimes opponents are relentless in their attacks. They get it into their heads that they should cause you grief and therefore try everything they can think of to oppose you. They keep at it day after day. That is when you desperately need to pray for God to protect you.

Malicious busybodies can cause you a great deal of pain when they take it on themselves to ruin your reputation or get others to shun you. And when they are popular or influential, their persecution amounts to oppression. They may be either open or discreet about their attacks, but the end result is the same.

David experienced this kind of oppression. Even though he was the king of Israel, he had many powerful foes whose tongues secretly worked like razors against him (Psalm 52:2). Read what he wrote in the Psalms and you will draw great comfort from it.

While you can and should speak up to defend your reputation and set the record straight, know that your best defense is prayer. God will be a shield to you and protect you.

BUT FOR GOD'S HELP

*If it had not been the L*ORD *who was on our side, when men rose up against us: then they had swallowed us up quick.*
PSALM 124:2–3 KJV

If you think about it, you can probably remember times when you came a hairbreadth away from disaster but were spared. This includes traffic collisions or financial calamity or times when vindictive people made you their target. These close brushes happen all too often.

You may wonder why God allows such a barrage of challenges. But it is the world and merciless enemies that mount constant attrition against you, not God. He steps in as your wall of protection, preventing the ongoing attacks from sweeping you away.

Still, you may become weary of all this and worry that one day God will fail to be there for you. David wavered at one point. He had been pursued for years by King Saul's armies and finally thought, "Someday Saul is going to get me" (1 Samuel 27:1 NLT).

But it never happened. So don't give up before the bell rings. God has your back. Stay faithful, and He won't allow your enemies to swallow you up.

FEELING OVERWHELMED

We were crushed and overwhelmed beyond our ability to endure, and we thought we would never live through it.

2 CORINTHIANS 1:8 NLT

Paul and his fellow workers went through really tough times. At one point, he candidly stated, "We were crushed and overwhelmed beyond our ability to endure." But you notice that he did endure, as did his companions. But had the situation continued, they wouldn't have.

God sometimes allows you to go through intolerable circumstances that, if they lasted much longer, would finish you. So Paul wasn't exaggerating when he thought he might not make it. He actually wouldn't have.

Some people harbor a niggling suspicion that God is cruel for allowing believers to go through such severe suffering and testing. But Paul put things in perspective when he said in that same Epistle, "For our light affliction, which is but for a moment, is working for us a far more exceeding and eternal weight of glory" (2 Corinthians 4:17 NKJV).

What at the moment is an unendurable crushing will be, in hindsight, "light affliction." You have to see the troubles of this life in the light of heaven to arrive at that conclusion.

SURVIVING OPPRESSION

"Many a time they have afflicted me from my youth;
yet they have not prevailed against me."
PSALM 129:2 NKJV

Some people have been picked on for as long as they can remember. Ever since they were little, people bullied them because of some disability—or over their weight or some other physical feature. This was hard to bear, but they refused to succumb, no matter how discouraged they became.

"Those were the hard times! Kicked around in public, targets of every kind of abuse. . . . Nothing they did bothered you, nothing set you back" (Hebrews 10:33–34 MSG). Perhaps you suffered this way, and the memories of it often do bother you. Some people become introverted and depressed over such treatment and even develop suicidal tendencies.

But you survived and became more empathetic and compassionate toward others who also suffered from bullies. Perhaps, though you wouldn't care to repeat the experience, it even made you stronger.

Christian life is often similar. Paul says, "It has been granted to you on behalf of Christ not only to believe in him, but also to suffer for him" (Philippians 1:29 NIV).

LIFE IS OFTEN DIFFICULT

"We must go through many hardships
to enter the kingdom of God."

ACTS 14:22 NIV

Sometimes God calls you to bear the almost unbearable. You might be asked to endure prolonged financial insecurity, a debilitating illness, or family turmoil.

You may ask God why, but even more worrying, you ask yourself if God has abandoned you. But take heart in what one Hebrew psalmist declared: "You, who have shown me great and severe troubles, shall revive me again" (Psalm 71:20 NKJV).

If God plans on delivering you and has "plans to give you hope and a future" (Jeremiah 29:11 NIV), you may ask why He lets you experience such trouble in the first place. Well, He knows that as painful as these testings can be, good can come from them. He told the Jews: "I have refined you, but not as silver is refined. Rather, I have refined you in the furnace of suffering" (Isaiah 48:10 NLT).

Jesus said, "Narrow is the gate and difficult is the way which leads to life" (Matthew 7:14 NKJV). He promised that His followers would experience hardships. It's the price you must pay to walk as Jesus walked.

WHEN SOMEONE SUES YOU

*"If you are sued in court and your shirt
is taken from you, give your coat, too."*
MATTHEW 5:40 NLT

Jesus said that if someone sued you for the shirt off your back, you were to let him have your coat as well. In saying this, Jesus was acknowledging that sometimes believers would lose court cases, and He advised giving more than the law required to show that you are living undefeated and trusting God to care for you.

Some people protest that giving away so much would leave you destitute, so Jesus couldn't have meant to do this literally. But the point remains: the legal system isn't necessarily the "justice system," so instead of being defeated by injustices when they happen, you must live victoriously.

Under Roman law, Christians had their entire properties and possessions confiscated! The Bible says, "When *all you owned* was taken from you, you accepted it with joy. You knew there were better things waiting for you that will last forever" (Hebrews 10:34 NLT, emphasis added).

Even if you lose in man's courts, be encouraged, for "great is your reward in heaven" (Matthew 5:12 KJV).

Church Discord

Scripture makes it clear that God has no patience with church arguments that spill over into gossip and backstabbing, factions and plots, outright lies and ever-accelerating hostility. It's all too easy to get sucked in—to take sides, to listen to the gossip, and even to contribute to the exaggeration and complaints that thrive in a divided church.

Conflicts are bound to happen in any family, including church families. But God's Spirit always seeks to heal and restore unity. As Christ's followers, we are called to be open to the Spirit leading us. . .to foster peace rather than strife!

*For first of all, when ye come together in the church,
I hear that there be divisions among you; and I
partly believe it. . . . Wherefore, my brethren, when
ye come together to eat, tarry one for another.*

1 CORINTHIANS 11:18, 33 KJV

*But we are to hold to the truth with love in our hearts.
We are to grow up and be more like Christ. He is the
leader of the church. Christ has put each part of the
church in its right place. Each part helps other parts.
This is what is needed to keep the whole body together.
In this way, the whole body grows strong in love.*

EPHESIANS 4:15–16 NLV

*Now I beseech you, brethren, by the name of our Lord Jesus
Christ, that ye all speak the same thing, and that there be no
divisions among you; but that ye be perfectly joined together
in the same mind and in the same judgment. For it hath been
declared unto me of you, my brethren, by them which are of
the house of Chloe, that there are contentions among you. Now
this I say, that every one of you saith, I am of Paul; and I of
Apollos; and I of Cephas; and I of Christ. Is Christ divided?*

1 CORINTHIANS 1:10–13 KJV

I urge you, brothers and sisters, to watch out for those who cause divisions and put obstacles in your way that are contrary to the teaching you have learned. Keep away from them.
ROMANS 16:17 NIV

God has put the body together. . .so that there should be no division in the body, but that its parts should have equal concern for each other. If one part suffers, every part suffers with it; if one part is honored, every part rejoices with it. Now you are the body of Christ, and each one of you is a part of it.
1 CORINTHIANS 12:24–27 NIV

Christ gave gifts to men. He gave to some the gift to be missionaries, some to be preachers, others to be preachers who go from town to town. He gave others the gift to be church leaders and teachers. These gifts help His people work well for Him. And then the church which is the body of Christ will be made strong.
EPHESIANS 4:11–12 NLV

"And I tell you, you are Peter, and on this rock I will build my church, and the gates of hell shall not prevail against it."
MATTHEW 16:18 ESV

These are grumblers, complainers, walking according to their own lusts; and they mouth great swelling words, flattering people to gain advantage. But you, beloved, remember the words which were spoken before by the apostles of our Lord Jesus Christ: how they told you that there would be mockers in the last time who would walk according to their own ungodly lusts. These are sensual persons, who cause divisions, not having the Spirit. But you, beloved, building yourselves up on your most holy faith, praying in the Holy Spirit, keep yourselves in the love of God, looking for the mercy of our Lord Jesus Christ unto eternal life.

JUDE 1:16–21 NKJV

God has put all things under Christ's power and has made Him to be the head leader over all things of the church. The church is the body of Christ. It is filled by Him Who fills all things everywhere with Himself.

EPHESIANS 1:22–23 NLV

*Bless those who persecute you; bless and do not curse them.
Rejoice with those who rejoice, weep with those who weep.
Live in harmony with one another. Do not be haughty,
but associate with the lowly. Never be wise in your
own sight. Repay no one evil for evil, but give thought
to do what is honorable in the sight of all. If possible,
so far as it depends on you, live peaceably with all.*
ROMANS 12:14–18 ESV

---

*Dear Lord, make me a peacemaker. Give me the
words to say what will build bridges between the
groups and individuals embroiled in conflict.*

EUODIA AND SYNTYCHE

*I plead with Euodia and I plead with Syntyche
to be of the same mind in the Lord.*

PHILIPPIANS 4:2 NIV

Paul had a deep love for the believers of Philippi. They had endured great persecution for their faith. They were generous and had faithfully supported his ministry. But he had to pause his praise at one point to give a shout-out to two women, Euodia ("sweet fragrance") and Syntyche ("fortunate"), who were allowing their disagreements to disrupt the church.

These were not two unspiritual busybodies, the kind of idle troublemakers you would expect to be involved in dissension. They were prominent women, companions of Paul, both active in God's work. In the next breath, Paul implores a church leader, "I ask you. . .help these women since they have contended at my side in the cause of the gospel" (Philippians 4:3 NIV).

Even the best of us sometimes collide with other believers, and at such times, may need help from spiritual leaders to sort out our quarrels. We won't always agree on all points, but we should "be of the same mind" regarding important issues such as love and unity.

HARMONY AND PEACE

Encourage each other. Live in harmony and peace.
Then the God of love and peace will be with you.
2 CORINTHIANS 13:11 NLT

Paul states an important fact: God is the "God of love and peace." You are probably already familiar with the famous statement that "God is love" (1 John 4:8 KJV), but it is important to realize that He is also the Spirit of peace. Wherever God is, there is peace.

Jesus said, "Where two or three are gathered together in My name, I am there in the midst of them" (Matthew 18:20 NKJV). Since Jesus is one with God the Father, where He is there is love and peace. This peace should be in evidence whenever Christians come together in His name. So it is only natural that believers encourage one another and live in harmony and tranquility.

Discord in the church could be avoided if Christians recognized that Jesus is personally present when they gather to worship, to hear the Word, and to fellowship. They must realize that the same Spirit of Christ present in their own life is present in other believers. To respect others is to respect Jesus.

REBELLING IN PRIDE

I wrote to the church, but Diotrephes, who loves to have the preeminence among them, does not receive us.

3 JOHN 1:9 NKJV

Often church discord is caused by nothing but pride. In his later years, the apostle John was based in Ephesus and oversaw the churches in the surrounding cities. Most Christians respected this great apostle and gladly listened to his instructions and admonitions.

But John was a simple man with a simple message and getting along in years—and a few local elders resented having to submit to him. They were well-to-do, educated, and eloquent, used to people respecting *them*. They loved being preeminent in their little kingdoms.

Unfortunately, some people today are like Diotrephes, and their pride causes problems and schisms in the church. But this isn't exceptional. We should all check our hearts: if we even have a slight touch of that attitude, it can cause us to resent godly leadership.

The Bible instructs us, "Have confidence in your leaders and submit to their authority, because they keep watch over you" (Hebrews 13:17 NIV). Be on guard against pride that would make you think you can ignore spiritual leaders.

CARNAL DIVISIONS

Whereas there is among you envying, and strife,
and divisions, are ye not carnal, and walk as men?
1 CORINTHIANS 3:3 KJV

A number of churches are plagued by doctrinal disagreements; people envy each other's jobs and positions; and strife, discord, and competition abound. Sometimes the divisions come out in the open as church splits. While people may give scriptural motives for their actions, often the reason is that they are simply lacking in love.

As Paul told the Corinthians, though they had experienced the life-changing power of God's Spirit, they were acting like carnal, unregenerate people who had never known God. So Paul advised them, "If we live in the Spirit, let us also walk in the Spirit" (Galatians 5:25 KJV). Let what is in your heart be made manifest in your outward actions.

Since "the love of God has been poured out in our hearts by the Holy Spirit" (Romans 5:5 NKJV), you should yield to the Holy Spirit and walk in that love. How do you avoid strife, divisions, and envy? "Walk in the Spirit, and you shall not fulfill the lust of the flesh" (Galatians 5:16 NKJV).

NECESSARY DISPUTES

*This brought Paul and Barnabas into
sharp dispute and debate with them.*
ACTS 15:2 NIV

Usually when disputes arise in a church, they are over doctrinal issues, church practices, or finances. Some people get stirred up emotionally and get argumentative over issues, while others want to just soothe the troubled waters and make all disagreements go away.

Some debates, however, are necessary. Certain doctrines are just plain wrong, many practices are inappropriate, and some financial decisions, if followed, would prove disastrous. But it is important to debate the issues in a loving manner and respectful tone, not in pride and anger, not impugning others' integrity or mocking their intelligence.

When certain Jews preached that Gentile believers had to become circumcised and keep Moses' law to be saved, Paul and Barnabas had a "sharp dispute and debate" with them. And they were right to do so. Jude advised Christians to "earnestly contend for the faith" (Jude 1:3 KJV).

But it is important that it is the issues that are sharply defined, not that the tones of voices are sharp. Even in a heated debate, Christians must be found "speaking the truth in love" (Ephesians 4:15 KJV).

Death of a Loved One

Our hearts are breaking inside us, and all the while we're forced to cope with day-to-day concerns. Emotionally, spiritually, and physically, we are in pain. Our lives will never be the same after losing a loved one.

There is no quick and easy way through this time. Grief has no shortcuts. But God has promised to be with us always. Nothing can separate us from His love—and He will walk with us, day by day and moment by moment, as we travel on grief's journey.

"Blessed are those who mourn,
for they shall be comforted."
MATTHEW 5:4 ESV

"I trust God for the same things they are looking
for. I am looking for the dead to rise."
ACTS 24:15 NLV

Weeping may endure for a night,
but joy comes in the morning.
PSALM 30:5 NKJV

"He will wipe away every tear from their eyes, and death
shall be no more, neither shall there be mourning, nor crying,
nor pain anymore, for the former things have passed away."
REVELATION 21:4 ESV

And provide for those who grieve in Zion—to bestow on them
a crown of beauty instead of ashes, the oil of joy instead of
mourning, and a garment of praise instead of a spirit of despair.
ISAIAH 61:3 NIV

Surely he hath borne our griefs,
and carried our sorrows.
ISAIAH 53:4 KJV

*"For sure, I tell you, you will cry and have sorrow,
but the world will have joy. You will have sorrow,
but your sorrow will turn into joy. . . . You are sad
now. I will see you again and then your hearts will
be full of joy. No one can take your joy from you."*

JOHN 16:20, 22 NLV

*Brothers and sisters, we do not want you to be uninformed
about those who sleep in death, so that you do not grieve like
the rest of mankind, who have no hope. For we believe that
Jesus died and rose again, and so we believe that God will
bring with Jesus those who have fallen asleep in him. According
to the Lord's word, we tell you that we who are still alive, who
are left until the coming of the Lord, will certainly not precede
those who have fallen asleep. For the Lord himself will come
down from heaven, with a loud command, with the voice of
the archangel and with the trumpet call of God, and the dead
in Christ will rise first. After that, we who are still alive and
are left will be caught up together with them in the clouds to
meet the Lord in the air. And so we will be with the Lord
forever. Therefore encourage one another with these words.*

1 THESSALONIANS 4:13–18 NIV

The LORD is near to those who have a broken heart.
PSALM 34:18 NKJV

*The lowly he sets on high, and those who
mourn are lifted to safety.*
JOB 5:11 NIV

*To everything there is a season, a time for every purpose under
heaven: a time to be born, and a time to die. . .a time to weep,
and a time to laugh; a time to mourn, and a time to dance.*
ECCLESIASTES 3:1–2, 4 NKJV

*My heart was grieved and my spirit embittered. . . . Yet I am
always with you; you hold me by my right hand. You guide me
with your counsel, and afterward you will take me into glory.*
PSALM 73:21, 23–24 NIV

*Be afflicted, and mourn, and weep: let your laughter be
turned to mourning, and your joy to heaviness. Humble
yourselves in the sight of the Lord, and he shall lift you up.*
JAMES 4:9–10 KJV

Rejoice with them that do rejoice,
and weep with them that weep.
ROMANS 12:15 KJV

"I will heal them; I will guide them and restore comfort
to Israel's mourners, creating praise on their lips.
Peace, peace, to those far and near," says the LORD.
ISAIAH 57:18–19 NIV

You have turned for me my mourning into dancing; you
have loosed my sackcloth and clothed me with gladness,
that my glory may sing your praise and not be silent.
O LORD my God, I will give thanks to you forever!
PSALM 30:11–12 ESV

I wasn't prepared for how much this would hurt,
Jesus. Please walk with me through my grief. Let me
allow this suffering to draw me closer to You.

MOURNING A CHILD

*"While the child was alive, I fasted
and wept. . . . But now he is dead."*
2 SAMUEL 12:22–23 NKJV

David had a child by Bathsheba, but he had committed adultery with her and had her husband murdered, so God told him that the child would die. When the infant became sick, David fasted and wept. But because God had made His will clear, David accepted the fact when the baby passed away.

Usually, however, the reasons for a child's death aren't clear, and you are left in grief, wondering why God took a child. Losing a child is a very painful experience. It's almost never a consequence of your sin, but you may feel that God has acted cruelly or without reason.

It's often easier to accept the death of a parent who has lived a full life than it is to see a child die before having an opportunity to experience what life on earth has to offer. One question burns in your mind: "Why?" And there usually doesn't seem to be an acceptable answer.

God understands your grief. But He also knows that you will have great joy when you are reunited with your child in heaven.

WHEN YOUR CHILD DIES

Some time later the woman's son became sick.
He grew worse and worse, and finally he died.
1 KINGS 17:17 NLT

Many a parent has passed sleepless nights watching over a child with a terminal illness. You endure agony as you watch them pass "through the valley of the shadow of death" (Psalm 23:4 KJV). And the pain is overwhelming when he or she finally leaves this life.

It's very difficult to say goodbye. And the days that follow have even more pain. You sit silently in his room, trying to grasp that he is truly gone. You arrange her toy animals on her bed, as if that might somehow make some sense of all the pain.

But try as you might, it makes no sense. What could be the purpose in taking such a beautiful child? But just as with Enoch, God has His reasons. "Enoch lived in close fellowship with God. . . .Then one day. . .God took him" (Genesis 5:22, 24 NLT).

Only time will heal your heartache—that and the knowledge that your child is now running through bright fields of splendor above, totally, unreservedly happy.

JAIRUS'S DAUGHTER

Weep not; she is not dead, but sleepeth.

LUKE 8:52 KJV

We all eventually die, and when someone's time has come to leave this life, we do well to accept it. But that isn't easy when the person whose time has come is very young and hasn't yet experienced all that life has to offer.

The New Testament records Jesus raising the dead on three occasions: He revived a young man, He brought a twelve-year-old girl back to life, and He raised his friend Lazarus (Luke 7:14–15; 8:51–55; John 11:38–44). Raising the dead was an exception, even for Jesus. Many hundreds of people died in Israel during the time of Jesus' ministry, and they didn't return.

But when someone dies with faith in Jesus, they live forever in His heavenly kingdom. This life is not the end, and the Bible refers to their temporary absence as "sleeping" (1 Corinthians 15:51; 1 Thessalonians 4:14). One day God will wake them, and their physical bodies will be resurrected in eternal life.

In that day, you and your departed child shall live together once again in rapturous joy.

WITH YOU A SHORT TIME

"Never again will there be in it an infant
who lives but a few days."

ISAIAH 65:20 NIV

Jesus once described a woman suffering the pains of labor: "When her child is born, her anguish gives way to joy because she has brought a new baby into the world" (John 16:21 NLT). After nine months of pregnancy, parents are delighted to welcome a new life.

But sometimes that joy is short lived. Even though the infant mortality rate is very low in the West, children still die in their first months. This raises painful questions: why was this new life given, only to be snatched away? And the inevitable question: what did I do wrong?

It's usually not that you did anything wrong. God isn't judging you for some sin. It's just that life is often hard. People in developing nations face this grim reality on a much more frequent basis. But one day such sorrow will be no more in all the earth.

During the coming reign of Christ on earth, "the child shall die one hundred years old" after living a full, happy life (Isaiah 65:20 NKJV).

THE PASSING OF A PARENT

I bowed down heavily, as one who mourns for his mother.
PSALM 35:14 NKJV

No matter how many signs you have of a parent's approaching death, even if he or she has been in failing health for years, the time of death can still come as a shock. It's the finality of it—knowing that you will never hear your father tell another corny joke or your mother express joy over another simple gift.

The grandfather clock still ticks away, but your parent's chair is now empty. Everywhere you look you find memories—from the photo albums, to the pictures on the walls, to the unfinished woodworking projects in his garage, to the half-knitted sweater in her sitting room.

Your mind is numb, and it takes the actual funeral for the reality to sink in that your parent is gone. Your days are filled with kind faces and gentle voices speaking condolences, but with every night come the emptiness and the tears.

You know your parent is with God now, and you know that must be incredibly beautiful, but you still need time to deal with your grief.

ON TO A HEAVENLY REWARD

Then he breathed his last and died at a ripe
old age, joining his ancestors in death.

GENESIS 35:29 NLT

Isaac lived to a great age, and when he passed away, his sons Esau and Jacob came to bury him. All his household mourned him. But Isaac had died "at a ripe old age," having lived a long, eventful life for God. The passing of this great man was as much an occasion to celebrate his legacy as it was to mourn his death.

Isaac had been fading for years—likely for decades—so his death came as no surprise. The passing away of your parents may be similar. They may even have had "a desire to depart and be with Christ" (Philippians 1:23 NKJV).

In fact, since Jesus opened the way to heaven, the demise of any born-again senior saint is cause for celebration. Although you will certainly miss your loved ones, it is comforting to know that if they loved the Lord they have gone on to a well-deserved reward. It's wonderful to realize that they are finally home, thronged by a company of great saints of ages past who have gone there before them.

GRIEVING A MOTHER

He married Rebekah and. . .he loved her.
So Isaac found comfort after his mother's death.
GENESIS 24:67 MSG

When Sarah died, Abraham mourned and wept bitter tears. But Abraham wasn't the only one in mourning. His son Isaac also grieved. He was the only son of his mother, and they'd had a special bond. So for months after her death, he found no comfort.

Abraham took another wife named Keturah, and he wisely realized that it was time that his son got married. So he sent a servant to Haran, and soon Rebekah came riding back in the camel caravan. After he was married, Isaac found solace, sweet companionship, and a sympathetic ear in Rebekah.

When your mother dies, you will probably feel emptiness within—even if you weren't as close to her as Isaac was to his mother. And though life must go on, there may be a mantle of grief draped over your days for some time.

Be sure to reach out to others who understand your sorrow and can sympathize and weep with you (Romans 12:15). It's important to process your grief, not bottle it all up inside.

A RIPE SHEAF OF GRAIN

"You shall come to the grave at a full age,
as a sheaf of grain ripens in its season."

JOB 5:26 NKJV

A long life lived for God is a beautiful thing. The departure to heaven of aged saints are joyful events. For when they finally arrive in their eternal home, they will hear, "Well done, good and faithful servant" (Matthew 25:21 NKJV).

The Bible describes the death of senior saints in delightful terms: if they die at a "full age," crowned with a head of white hair, scripture says they are like a sheaf of grain that has ripened at the end of the long summer season. Then the long-awaited harvest comes and they are taken home. Of course, their passing is bittersweet for those left behind, but death for a Christian is not the end.

It's right and proper to mourn the passing of an elderly believer, but it is also appropriate to celebrate a life well lived and to focus on the legacy the person leaves. This is true even if the person didn't accomplish "great" things but was simply a faithful husband or wife and a loving grandparent.

ONE LITTLE EWE LAMB

*"The poor man had nothing except one little
ewe lamb. . . . It was like a daughter to him."*
2 SAMUEL 12:3 NIV

A prophet once told David a story about a man who kept
a lamb as a house pet. "He raised it, and it grew up with
him and his children. It shared his food, drank from his cup
and even slept in his arms. It was like a daughter to him"
(2 Samuel 12:3 NIV). David was overcome with emotion
when he learned that the lamb had been killed.

People have had tender feelings for pets for thousands of
years and have felt keen grief when they die. Some modern
people shake their head in disbelief when their grieving
mother laments the death of her dog. But God created animals capable of expressing affection, and He understands.

Do animals go to heaven? Many may do so. Revelation
19:11, 14 tell us there are horses in paradise. And Isaiah
65:17, 25 describes animals such as wolves, sheep, lions,
cattle, and snakes there. Dogs aren't specifically mentioned,
but we can safely assume that if wolves are there, dogs will
be there as well.

A FOUR-FOOTED FRIEND

"Even the little dogs eat the crumbs
which fall from their masters' table."
MATTHEW 15:27 NKJV

Dogs weren't looked on with much fondness in ancient Israel. Although some served as sheepdogs, most were simply strays wandering the streets of the city in packs, foraging through garbage, growling at people who got too close. So the Old Testament doesn't share a great deal of tender sentiments about dogs.

But by New Testament times, they had been fully accepted as pets, were often small breeds like the "little dogs" referred to in Matthew 15:27, and had made their way into people's hearts and homes. They frequently lay under the table at their masters' feet, eating the scraps that dropped. A Phoenician woman made reference of this fact to Jesus.

Dogs experience love, happiness, and other emotions just like people, and as they develop closer bonds, each often mourns the other's passing. Dogs experience genuine grief when their masters die, and people often feel pangs of sorrow when their dogs die.

Don't be ashamed to grieve when your four-footed companion passes away. God has a tender spot in His heart for His creations as well.

LOSS OF A PARTNER

Then Elimelech died, and Naomi
was left with her two sons.
RUTH 1:3 NLT

Once when there was a long famine in Israel, Naomi and her husband sold their land to buy food; then they left Bethlehem for Moab, where they found some relief for a few years. There Naomi's husband died. Naomi was grief-stricken, and none of her relatives and former neighbors were present to comfort her.

To make matters worse, her two sons died also. This left her financially destitute. A devastated widow, she decided to return to Israel. As she went, she lamented, "The LORD's hand has turned against me!" (Ruth 1:13 NIV).

Many people down through the centuries have identified with Naomi's feelings of despair. It is very difficult to lose a life partner. And it is worse when you have to take over your deceased spouse's duties and handle the finances.

But we know the end of Naomi's story: God showed her tender compassion. Her daughter-in-law Ruth returned with her to Judah, married a wealthy landowner, and cared for her. Naomi had thought that God had abandoned her. . . but He hadn't. He hasn't abandoned you either.

MOURNING A LIFE COMPANION

Sarah died. . .and Abraham came to mourn
for Sarah, and to weep for her.
GENESIS 23:2 KJV

Sarah lived for 127 years, so she and Abraham had been married for about 110 years. Sarah was very beautiful and maintained her lovely features into her senior years. We know this because the king of Gerar desired to marry her when she was ninety (Genesis 17:17; 20:1–2).

When Sarah died, Abraham wept openly. She had been his closest companion for over a century. Then, cloaked in his grief, he took care of funeral arrangements. It was at this time that he bought the cave of Machpelah for a family tomb (Genesis 23).

When your life's companion dies, it seems that part of you dies as well. You had "become one" in marriage, and your physical beings, emotions, and habits had become almost inextricably intertwined, so much so that you can be at a loss as to how you will cope. This is different from the loss of a friend or even a family member.

At such times, the knowledge that you will see your loved one again in heaven gives steady light for your path.

THE DESIRE OF YOUR EYES

*"Behold, I take away from you the desire
of your eyes with one stroke."*
EZEKIEL 24:16 NKJV

Ezekiel was a young priest, and like many other Jewish captives, he was living in exile in Babylon. But he had one consolation: he was very happily married and his wife was "the desire of his eyes." Then one morning God warned Ezekiel that He was about to take her.

The Bible doesn't indicate whether Ezekiel's wife was already sick from a lingering disease—and whether she took a turn for the worse, prompting this revelation—or whether she suffered from a sudden, unexpected stroke. But that same evening she died.

God gave Ezekiel a very unusual command, instructing him not to mourn outwardly, but to "sigh in silence" (Ezekiel 24:17 NKJV). And Ezekiel obeyed. If his wife had been sick for many months, this would have given him time to prepare for her eventual demise, but still, Ezekiel would have been very heavyhearted.

It is especially difficult when your spouse dies young, in the prime of life. God understands your sorrow and expects you to grieve. His command to Ezekiel was a rare exception.

Depression

Depression is more than just the daily sadnesses that come and go. It's a deep-seated feeling that grabs hold of us and doesn't let go, day after day. It can take a toll on our social lives, our professional lives, our spiritual lives, and our health.

As Christians we may feel we should be immune to depression. But depression is no sin! God has promised us He will be especially close to us when we go through these bleak times. He will be there at our side, waiting to lead us into His joy once more.

*Blessed be the God and Father of our Lord Jesus Christ,
the Father of mercies and God of all comfort.*
2 CORINTHIANS 1:3 ESV

*Shout for joy, you heavens; rejoice, you earth; burst into
song, you mountains! For the LORD comforts his people
and will have compassion on his afflicted ones.*
ISAIAH 49:13 NIV

*The LORD is close to the brokenhearted and
saves those who are crushed in spirit.*
PSALM 34:18 NIV

*Answer me speedily, O LORD; my spirit fails!
Do not hide Your face from me, lest I be like those
who go down into the pit. Cause me to hear Your
lovingkindness in the morning, for in You do I trust.*
PSALM 143:7–8 NKJV

*"He found him in a desert land, and in the howling
waste of the wilderness; he encircled him, he cared
for him, he kept him as the apple of his eye."*
DEUTERONOMY 32:10 ESV

He heals the brokenhearted and binds up their wounds.

PSALM 147:3 NIV

*I waited patiently for the L*ORD*; and He inclined to me, and heard my cry. He also brought me up out of a horrible pit, out of the miry clay, and set my feet upon a rock, and established my steps. He has put a new song in my mouth—praise to our God.*

PSALM 40:1–3 NKJV

Why are you cast down, O my soul? And why are you disquieted within me? Hope in God; for I shall yet praise Him, the help of my countenance and my God.

PSALM 42:11 NKJV

In the beginning was the Word, and the Word was with God, and the Word was God. He was in the beginning with God. All things were made through him, and without him was not any thing made that was made. In him was life, and the life was the light of men. The light shines in the darkness, and the darkness has not overcome it.

JOHN 1:1–5 ESV

135

"Until now you have not asked for anything in My name. Ask and you will receive. Then your joy will be full."

JOHN 16:24 NLV

Bear one another's burdens, and so fulfill the law of Christ.

GALATIANS 6:2 ESV

Blessed be God, even the Father of our Lord Jesus Christ, the Father of mercies, and the God of all comfort; who comforteth us in all our tribulation, that we may be able to comfort them which are in any trouble, by the comfort wherewith we ourselves are comforted of God.

2 CORINTHIANS 1:3–4 KJV

"He reached down from on high and took hold of me; he drew me out of deep waters. He rescued me from my powerful enemy, from my foes, who were too strong for me. They confronted me in the day of my disaster, but the LORD was my support. He brought me out into a spacious place; he rescued me because he delighted in me."

2 SAMUEL 22:17–20 NIV

"And you, child, will be called the prophet of the Most High; for you will go before the Lord to prepare his ways, to give knowledge of salvation to his people. . .because of the tender mercy of our God, whereby the sunrise shall visit us from on high to give light to those who sit in darkness and in the shadow of death, to guide our feet into the way of peace."

LUKE 1:76–79 ESV

But You, O LORD, are a shield for me, my glory
and the One who lifts up my head.

PSALM 3:3 NKJV

"You are sad now. I will see you again and then your hearts
will be full of joy. No one can take your joy from you."

JOHN 16:22 NLV

I'm waiting patiently for You, Lord. I know You will lean
down to me and hear my cry. You will draw me up out of
this miry bog of depression where I'm stuck. You will set my
feet on the rock and make my steps steady. And then You
will put a new song in my mouth, a song of praise to God.

REFUSING TO DESPAIR

We are pressed on every side by troubles, but we are not crushed. We are perplexed, but not driven to despair.

2 CORINTHIANS 4:8 NLT

The apostle Paul endured unbelievable hardships yet kept a positive outlook. In Philippi, he and Silas were cruelly beaten and thrown into prison. Instead of complaining, they sang praise to God (Acts 16:22–25). Paul refused to give in to despair and later advised the persecuted Philippian believers, "Rejoice in the Lord always. Again I will say, rejoice!" (Philippians 4:4 NKJV).

Many modern Christians, however, suffer from depression, and though they battle it and seek to stay positive, they are not always successful. Instead of berating them for being too weak to maintain a victorious attitude, we should commend them for their efforts and encourage them to continue trusting God.

If you suffer from clinical depression, you may sometimes feel helpless to rise above dark waves of depression. Don't feel condemned if you need to take medication to adjust a chemical imbalance in your brain.

At the same time, aggressively strive to be positive—soaking your thoughts in God's Word, listening to praise and worship music, and constantly quoting faith-building promises from scripture.

REASON TO LIVE

"What strength do I have, that I should hope?
And what is my end, that I should prolong my life?"
JOB 6:11 NKJV

Depression can have many causes, but when it comes, it can sap your will to live. You don't feel like doing anything. Everything seems hopeless. And sometimes there may not be much you can do—particularly if you have a physical disability that leaves you bedridden or with little strength.

You may wonder why you should continue to hope. What strength do you have to act even if an opportunity was to open? What is God's plan, what end does He have in mind, that you should continue hoping? What could He possibly still have for you to accomplish, given the state you are in?

If you feel there is no reason to live, you may desire to depart for heaven before God is done with you on earth. But God doesn't see the way people see. What to you may seem like large, meaningful accomplishments—causes well worth living for—may have little significance to God. But small, everyday acts that seem almost insignificant to you may be vitally important to Him.

A CRUSHED SPIRIT

My heart is smitten, and withered like grass;
so that I forget to eat my bread.
PSALM 102:4 KJV

You can bear up under great adversity as long as you have hope. You can suffer setbacks and sicknesses or endure rejection as long as you keep your spirits up. But once you lose hope, you succumb to depression. "The human spirit can endure in sickness, but a crushed spirit who can bear?" (Proverbs 18:14 NIV).

The Bible tells us that "a broken spirit dries the bones" (Proverbs 17:22 NKJV). Sometimes you feel hopeless and dispirited. And when this happens, you have no will to continue. You are unable to go on.

If you are suffering from depression, the source of your pain may be a broken spirit. Life has battered you badly, shaken your trust in God, and drained your will to continue. And if you had a preexisting disposition to depression, it has hit you all the harder.

Rest in the Lord and let Him renew you. Meditate on His Word and draw strength from His promises. Allow His gentle hands to mend your wounds and restore your confidence.

A BROKEN SPIRIT

The spirit of a man will sustain him in sickness,
but who can bear a broken spirit?
PROVERBS 18:14 NKJV

If you have faith in God, it will keep you going even when you are sick. But if you lose all hope, if your spirit is weak and broken, nothing remains to sustain you. Then you are left with depression.

Many Christians mistakenly think that God wants them to be desperate, broken, and weeping, for they wrongly translate David's words, "The LORD is close to the brokenhearted and saves those who are crushed in spirit" (Psalm 34:18 NIV). However, He draws near you to heal your broken spirit and comfort you—not to make you broken.

Throughout the Scriptures, being broken means being shattered (Jeremiah 19:1–2, 10–11) and crushed and weak (Proverbs 15:13; 17:22). Breaking is what happens to dry, brittle, hardened vessels that can no longer be changed, for whom there is no more hope.

But if you are a moist, soft clay vessel, still trusting God, still on the Potter's wheel, He allows pressure to mold and shape you. This pressure may be painful at times, but it leads to godly change, not hopelessness and depression.

A COMFORTING FRIEND

*It was a beautiful thing that you came
alongside me in my troubles.*
PHILIPPIANS 4:14 MSG

Many people don't have an actual case of clinical depression; nevertheless, they feel down and depressed. Perhaps life has dealt them a series of hard blows that have dampened their spirits and weighed them down. Or perhaps there is a cloud over their days because of worries about their health, their finances, or their families.

Taking the time to speak encouraging words to them can be a huge help. Solomon said, "Anxiety in the heart of man causes depression, but a good word makes it glad" (Proverbs 12:25 NKJV).

You may hesitate to try to encourage someone. You may think that you won't know what to say, that you will come off sounding awkward, or that your words won't have any effect. Go ahead and do it anyway. Your friend will probably appreciate that you cared enough to try.

Sometimes just coming alongside someone helps, even if you don't have great words of wisdom to impart. They will be glad to know that you are thinking about them and praying for them.

Disabilities

The Gospels are full of stories of Jesus healing people. We never hear of Him looking down on these people as being less important or less deserving of His time. Instead, He treated each one with respect and compassion—and then He raised them up.

As Christ's followers, we too are called to reach out to those with disabilities. We cannot heal their physical issues—but we can treat them with dignity and respect. We can make sure they are not overlooked or ignored. And we can work to bring them back into society, allowing them to contribute to our communities.

His followers asked Him, "Teacher, whose sin made this man to be born blind? Was it the sin of this man or the sin of his parents?" Jesus answered, "The sin of this man or the sin of his parents did not make him to be born blind. He was born blind so the work of God would be seen in him. We must keep on doing the work of Him Who sent Me while it is day. Night is coming when no man can work. While I am in the world, I am the Light of the world."

JOHN 9:2–5 NLV

After you have suffered for awhile, God Himself will make you perfect. He will keep you in the right way. He will give you strength. He is the God of all loving-favor and has called you through Christ Jesus to share His shining-greatness forever.

1 PETER 5:10 NLV

And if the ear should say, "Because I am not an eye, I do not belong to the body," it would not for that reason stop being part of the body. If the whole body were an eye, where would the sense of hearing be? . . . God has placed the parts in the body, every one of them, just as he wanted them to be.

1 CORINTHIANS 12:16–18 NIV

*"You shall not curse the deaf or put a stumbling block before the blind, but you shall fear your God: I am the L*ORD.*"*
LEVITICUS 19:14 ESV

Then Jesus said to his host, "When you give a luncheon or dinner, do not invite your friends, your brothers or sisters, your relatives, or your rich neighbors; if you do, they may invite you back and so you will be repaid. But when you give a banquet, invite the poor, the crippled, the lame, the blind, and you will be blessed."
LUKE 14:12–14 NIV

*The L*ORD *said to him, "Who gave human beings their mouths? Who makes them deaf or mute? Who gives them sight or makes them blind? Is it not I, the L*ORD*?"*
EXODUS 4:11 NIV

Not only so, but we also glory in our sufferings, because we know that suffering produces perseverance; perseverance, character; and character, hope. And hope does not put us to shame, because God's love has been poured out into our hearts through the Holy Spirit, who has been given to us.
ROMANS 5:3–5 NIV

*But he said to me, "My grace is sufficient for you, for
my power is made perfect in weakness." Therefore
I will boast all the more gladly of my weaknesses,
so that the power of Christ may rest upon me.*
2 CORINTHIANS 12:9 ESV

*Jesus answered and said unto them, Go and shew John
again those things which ye do hear and see: the blind
receive their sight, and the lame walk, the lepers are
cleansed, and the deaf hear, the dead are raised up,
and the poor have the gospel preached to them.*
MATTHEW 11:4–5 KJV

*The eye cannot say to the hand, "I have no need of you," nor
again the head to the feet, "I have no need of you." On the
contrary, the parts of the body that seem to be weaker are
indispensable, and on those parts of the body that we think less
honorable we bestow the greater honor. . . . God has so composed
the body, giving greater honor to the part that lacked it, that
there may be no division in the body, but that the members may
have the same care for one another. If one member suffers, all
suffer together; if one member is honored, all rejoice together.*
1 CORINTHIANS 12:21–26 ESV

For You formed my inward parts; You covered me in my mother's womb. I will praise You, for I am fearfully and wonderfully made; marvelous are Your works, and that my soul knows very well.

PSALM 139:13–14 NKJV

Wherefore lift up the hands which hang down, and the feeble knees; and make straight paths for your feet, lest that which is lame be turned out of the way; but let it rather be healed.

HEBREWS 12:12–13 KJV

For we are his workmanship, created in Christ Jesus for good works, which God prepared beforehand, that we should walk in them.

EPHESIANS 2:10 ESV

We know that God makes all things work together for the good of those who love Him and are chosen to be a part of His plan.

ROMANS 8:28 NLV

Dear Father, may I see You in each person, no matter how broken they may appear to be on the outside. May I remember that when I serve those who are disabled, I am truly serving You.

147

WHEN CHILDREN
HAVE DISABILITIES

His nurse picked him up and fled, but as she
hurried to leave, he fell and became disabled.
2 SAMUEL 4:4 NIV

It's difficult to understand why babies are born with disabilities. It's just as difficult to understand why God allows young children to suffer disease or accidents that leave them disabled for life. This causes parents to ask, "Why *her*, God? What did this innocent child ever do to deserve this?"

The answer is that the child didn't "deserve" it, but diseases and accidents are no respecters of persons, and even children aren't spared. So they are born blind, deaf, and disabled, and while this causes the parents grief and soul-searching at first, they eventually accept their children's limitations and learn to encourage them to reach their full potential just the same.

But don't forget: God will one day utterly change them. Their present bodies may be weak or disabled, but when His kingdom comes, their bodies will be transformed and made powerful and eternal. "Our bodies are buried in brokenness, but they will be raised in glory. They are buried in weakness, but they will be raised in strength" (1 Corinthians 15:43 NLT).

CARING FOR THOSE
WITH DISABILITIES

"When you give a banquet, invite the poor, the crippled,
the lame, the blind, and you will be blessed."

LUKE 14:13–14 NIV

You may observe people gently caring for those with physical or mental disabilities and think, *So much love! I could never do that.* You may admire their dedication but not be able to imagine rolling up your sleeves and caring for those with disabilities yourself.

But caring for the poor, the disabled, the lame, the blind, and the mentally challenged can often be part of living the Gospel. Jesus cares for them, and He tells you who follow Him to help the disadvantaged: "Whenever you did one of these things to someone overlooked or ignored, that was me—you did it to me" (Matthew 25:40 MSG).

Such loving actions begin at home—caring for a family member with disabilities, feeding an elderly parent, spending time talking with a shut-in relative who tells you the same stories every time you visit.

If you yourself are disabled, you know how much such care and acts of kindness mean. So go the extra mile and show the same love to those less fortunate than you.

LEVITES WITH DISABILITIES

"No man who has any defect may come near:
no man who is blind or lame, disfigured or deformed."
LEVITICUS 21:18 NIV

The law of Moses stated that no Levite who was "blind or lame, disfigured or deformed" could offer food to God on His altar. Some readers therefore conclude that God thinks less of those with disabilities, and they wonder why a God of love would reject the human beings with disabilities whom He Himself formed.

But God's love and care extend to those with disabilities, for in the same passage, the Lord said, "He may eat the most holy food of his God, as well as the holy food; yet because of his defect, he must not. . .approach the altar" (Leviticus 21:22–23 NIV).

Levites with disabilities could eat the food dedicated to God Almighty, including "the most holy food"—which was off limits to the vast majority of Israelites. God did not care less for them just because they weren't permitted to do everything able-bodied Levites did.

And now that Christ has opened the way to the Father, this restriction is past, and God's disabled children freely approach His throne of grace.

HEALING AND HELPING

He looked up and said,
"I see men like trees, walking."

MARK 8:24 NKJV

When Jesus came to Bethsaida, people brought a blind man to Him. Instead of immediately healing him, Jesus led him away from the crowds. Then He spit on his eyes, placed His hands on him, and asked him if he saw anything.

The man replied, "I see men like trees, walking." So Jesus placed His hands on the man's eyes again and made him look up. This time he saw everyone clearly. These days if someone saw men that blurry, most Christians would refer him to the optometrist.

In fact, medical missionaries, lacking the ability to miraculously heal the visually impaired, equip them with glasses or perform eye operations to correct their vision. And instead of healing paraplegics, practical Christians motivated by love provide wheelchairs to give them mobility.

It's great if you have the faith to heal the blind, the paralyzed, and the disabled, but few Christians actually have faith like that. But we should all have the love of Christ. And remember, it is even more important to have love than the faith to work miracles (1 Corinthians 13:2, 13).

GOD'S CHILDREN
WITH DISABILITIES

*"Who makes the mute, the deaf, the seeing,
or the blind? Have not I, the LORD?"*

EXODUS 4:11 NKJV

You may have proclaimed this verse when a baby was born: "I praise you because I am fearfully and wonderfully made; your works are wonderful" (Psalm 139:14 NIV). But are God's works still wonderful when a child is born blind or with another imperfection? Yes, they are.

You may wonder what purpose the Lord has in creating the mute, the deaf, and the blind. But you do well to remember that all human beings are imperfect in one way or another—often in many ways. What is God's purpose in creating us?

Well, our lives owe much of their significance to how we affect others. People with disabilities have a powerful effect on people. They present countless opportunities to others to show compassion. When you love and help others, you fulfill Christ's law. "Carry each other's burdens, and in this way you will fulfill the law of Christ" (Galatians 6:2 NIV).

When we get to heaven, we will see how backward we had so many of our priorities, for "the last shall be first" (Matthew 19:30 KJV).

Disappointment

Disappointment comes in all shapes and sizes. Maybe life itself has disappointed us. Maybe someone we counted on has let us down. Or maybe we have disappointed ourselves. Our own failures and weaknesses have forced us to realize that we're not the people we dreamed of being.

But one thing is certain: no matter what else disappoints us, God never will! When everything else lets us down—when the fig tree doesn't bud, the vines have no grapes, our crops fail, and everything in our lives is empty—we can still rejoice in God our Savior.

Though the fig tree should not blossom, nor fruit be on the vines, the produce of the olive fail and the fields yield no food, the flock be cut off from the fold and there be no herd in the stalls, yet I will rejoice in the LORD; I will take joy in the God of my salvation.

HABAKKUK 3:17–18 ESV

"You will know that I am the LORD; those who hope in me will not be disappointed."

ISAIAH 49:23 NIV

Now to Him who is able to do exceedingly abundantly above all that we ask or think, according to the power that works in us, to Him be glory in the church by Christ Jesus to all generations, forever and ever.

EPHESIANS 3:20–21 NKJV

I have learned to be content whatever the circumstances. I know what it is to be in need, and I know what it is to have plenty. I have learned the secret of being content in any and every situation, whether well fed or hungry, whether living in plenty or in want. I can do all this through him who gives me strength.

PHILIPPIANS 4:11–13 NIV

Now listen, you who say, "Today or tomorrow we will go to this or that city, spend a year there, carry on business and make money." Why, you do not even know what will happen tomorrow. What is your life? You are a mist that appears for a little while and then vanishes. Instead, you ought to say, "If it is the Lord's will, we will live and do this or that."

JAMES 4:13–15 NIV

But if we have food and clothing, we will be content with that.

1 TIMOTHY 6:8 NIV

My Christian brothers, you should be happy when you have all kinds of tests. You know these prove your faith. It helps you not to give up. Learn well how to wait so you will be strong and complete and in need of nothing.

JAMES 1:2-4 NLV

Now hope does not disappoint, because the love of God has been poured out in our hearts by the Holy Spirit who was given to us.

ROMANS 5:5 NKJV

Now the Lord of All says, "Think about your ways! You have planted much, but gather little. You eat, but there is not enough to fill you. You drink, but never have your fill. You put on clothing, but no one is warm enough. You earn money, but put it into a bag with holes."... And the people honored the Lord with fear. Then Haggai the man of God spoke for the Lord to the people, saying, "I am with you," says the Lord.

HAGGAI 1:5–6, 12–13 NLV

My soul will be satisfied as with fat and rich food,
and my mouth will praise you with joyful lips.

PSALM 63:5 ESV

But he said to me, "My grace is sufficient for you."

2 CORINTHIANS 12:9 ESV

So do not fear, for I am with you; do not be dismayed,
for I am your God. I will strengthen you and help you;
I will uphold you with my righteous right hand.

ISAIAH 41:10 NIV

The fear of the LORD leads to life; then one rests content, untouched by trouble.

PROVERBS 19:23 NIV

Hope deferred makes the heart sick, but when the desire comes, it is a tree of life.

PROVERBS 13:12 NKJV

As for me, I shall behold your face in righteousness; when I awake, I shall be satisfied with your likeness.

PSALM 17:15 ESV

Lord, when I reach the point where I have nothing left but You, I can finally realize that You alone are enough. All my questions won't be answered in this life. My circumstances may not be improved. I'll have to let go of some of the things I've set my heart on. But none of that matters. You are the strength of my heart and my portion forever.

UNRELENTING DISAPPOINTMENT

Unrelenting disappointment leaves you heartsick,
but a sudden good break can turn life around.

PROVERBS 13:12 MSG

God knows that relentless disappointment leaves you mentally exhausted. After a while, you begin to get the feeling that nothing good will ever come your way again. You are overcome with futility.

You may feel like Job whose friends tried to encourage him that if he would hang in there, just persevere, that God would eventually bless him again (Job 4:3–7; 8:6, 21). God would "restore to you the years that the. . .locust has eaten" (Joel 2:25 NKJV).

But like Job, you may have nearly given up hope that this will ever happen. When the locusts have devoured so many years of your life and you are persuaded that God Himself is intent on causing you grief, it is difficult to think that it will ever seem like a good idea to Him to bless you again.

But this time of testing and disappointment won't last forever. It too will pass. God loves you and is determined to do good in your life. Like the sun bursting through the clouds, He will completely change your situation and give you hope again.

DEALING WITH DISAPPOINTMENT

"The brook vanishes in the heat. The caravans turn aside to be refreshed, but there is nothing to drink."

JOB 6:17–18 NLT

In Bible lands, intermittent brooks—called *wadis*—run with water only after the spring rains. Then, as the long, hot summer months stretch on, the streambeds dry up. Soon water is to be found only in a few small pools. Many a caravan has stopped at a wadi, desperate for water, to find nothing at all.

Perhaps you have experienced similar disappointment: You were depending on a job to come through. You had exhausted all your other resources and had no backup plan. You needed this to happen. Yet it fell through, and you were bitterly disheartened.

What can you do? The Bible describes the arid valley of Baca. *Baca* means "weeping" and symbolizes times of great disappointment. Yet God's people "passing through the valley of Baca make it a well" (Psalm 84:6 KJV). When you desperately need water but there is none in sight, that is when you must dig a well.

God will never fail you, but sometimes you need to dig deep in a place of disappointment to find hope.

WHEN HOPES ARE DASHED

They count on it but are disappointed.
When they arrive, their hopes are dashed.

JOB 6:20 NLT

When you are counting on someone to help you but the time comes and your would-be helper bails out, your hopes are dashed. Maybe he promised to lend you money to meet an unexpected shortfall, or she said she would drive you to an appointment, but then the person doesn't come through.

God knows what it is like to be disappointed. He compared His care for Israel to a farmer painstakingly preparing the ground, removing stones, and planting a vineyard. Yet the vine produced bitter grapes. God asked, "What more could have been done to My vineyard that I have not done in it? Why then, when I expected it to bring forth good grapes, did it bring forth wild grapes?" (Isaiah 5:4 NKJV).

People continue to disappoint God today, yet He patiently, lovingly continues to work in their lives. "For He knows our frame; He remembers that we are dust" (Psalm 103:14 NKJV).

When your hopes fall through, look to God to comfort you and meet your needs. He will come through for you when people fail.

HOPE THAT NEVER DISAPPOINTS

This hope will not lead to disappointment.
For we know how dearly God loves us.

ROMANS 5:5 NLT

We all have had high hopes at times and have had our hearts set on something, only to be disappointed. People forget their promises or thoughtlessly fail to keep their word, and even "sure deals" fall through. Problems and trials seem to be woven right into the fabric of life and are constantly upsetting our carefully made plans.

But Paul said that it is not only possible to endure when you run into problems, but to rejoice, because trials develop godly character. This development process strengthens your confident hope of salvation, and such hope will never lead to disappointment.

Sometimes it is helpful to take a deep breath, pause for a moment, and see disappointments in perspective. This life is full of frustrations and failures, but through them all, God works everything for good and will more than make up for your losses in heaven.

You can be certain of this, knowing how much God loves you. This love is what moves Him to have so many wonderful things planned and waiting for you. And God never disappoints.

DISAPPOINTING RETURNS

"You looked for much, but indeed it came to little."

HAGGAI 1:9 NKJV

How many times have you launched out on a new venture with high hopes, only to have your hopes dashed? Many times, if you are an entrepreneur. This can be very upsetting after putting your all into something.

You realize that in the past you have gone off half-cocked, so this time you do lots of research, come up with a truly winning idea, and carefully plan all the details—only to fail again.

As the prophet Haggai explained, this often happens if you don't put God and His purposes first. As a result, He isn't with you to bless you. But it can also happen for inscrutable marketing reasons, and often there is no way to accurately predict what will succeed. The Bible says, "For you do not know which will prosper, either this or that" (Ecclesiastes 11:6 NKJV).

As Solomon noted, "The race is not to the swift. . .nor riches to men of understanding, nor favor to men of skill; but time and chance happen to them all" (Ecclesiastes 9:11 NKJV). Often that is just the way things are.

Dishonesty

As Christ's followers, we are to believe the truth, love the truth, and walk in the truth. We are to speak the truth in love. Christ came to us full of grace and truth, but He went still further than that: He told us that He *is* the Truth personified, the Truth incarnate. We are to love the truth because Jesus is the Truth. We are to stay close to it and follow after it, because that is the way we follow our Lord. If we are Christ's representatives, then those around us should know we always speak the truth.

*And the Word became flesh and dwelt among us,
and we have seen his glory, glory as of the only
Son from the Father, full of grace and truth.*

JOHN 1:14 ESV

*As for me, You hold me up in my honesty.
And You set me beside You forever.*

PSALM 41:12 NLV

*Therefore, having put away falsehood, let each one of you speak
the truth with his neighbor, for we are members one of another.*

EPHESIANS 4:25 ESV

*A wicked person earns deceptive wages, but the one
who sows righteousness reaps a sure reward.*

PROVERBS 11:18 NIV

*Therefore seeing we have this ministry, as we have received
mercy, we faint not; but have renounced the hidden things of
dishonesty, not walking in craftiness, nor handling the word of
God deceitfully; but by manifestation of the truth commending
ourselves to every man's conscience in the sight of God.*

2 CORINTHIANS 4:1–2 KJV

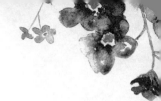

The Lord hates a false weight, but a true weight is His joy.
PROVERBS 11:1 NLV

*Dishonest money dwindles away, but whoever
gathers money little by little makes it grow.*
PROVERBS 13:11 NIV

*"Whoever can be trusted with very little can also be
trusted with much, and whoever is dishonest with
very little will also be dishonest with much."*
LUKE 16:10 NIV

*The Lord hates lying lips, but those who
speak the truth are His joy.*
PROVERBS 12:22 NLV

*Hear this, you who trample the needy and do away with the
poor of the land, saying, "When will the New Moon be over
that we may sell grain, and the Sabbath be ended that we
may market wheat?"—skimping on the measure, boosting
the price and cheating with dishonest scales, buying the poor
with silver and the needy for a pair of sandals, selling even the
sweepings with the wheat. The LORD has sworn by himself, the
Pride of Jacob: "I will never forget anything they have done."*
AMOS 8:4–7 NIV

Be careful to do what is right in the eyes of everyone.
ROMANS 12:17 NIV

*These are the things you shall do: speak each
man the truth to his neighbor; give judgment
in your gates for truth, justice, and peace.*
ZECHARIAH 8:16 NKJV

*The lip of truth shall be established for ever:
but a lying tongue is but for a moment.*
PROVERBS 12:19 KJV

*"You have heard that it was said long ago, 'You must not
make a promise you cannot keep. You must carry out your
promises to the Lord.' I tell you, do not use strong words when
you make a promise. Do not promise by heaven. It is the place
where God is. Do not promise by earth. It is where He rests
His feet. . . . Do not promise by your head. You are not able to
make one hair white or black. Let your yes be YES. Let your
no be NO. Anything more than this comes from the devil."*
MATTHEW 5:33–37 NLV

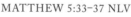

For we aim at what is honorable not only in the Lord's sight but also in the sight of man.

2 CORINTHIANS 8:21 ESV

Blessed are they that do his commandments, that they may have right to the tree of life, and may enter in through the gates into the city. For without are dogs, and sorcerers, and whoremongers, and murderers, and idolaters, and whosoever loveth and maketh a lie.

REVELATION 22:14–15 KJV

Teach me thy way, O LORD; I will walk in thy truth: unite my heart to fear thy name.

PSALM 86:11 KJV

God, I know You never lie, for You are the God of truth. I can trust You never to be dishonest with me. You always keep Your promises. But Your Son called Satan a "liar and the father of lies." (John 8:44 NIV). Remind me always that when I speak the truth, I am speaking Your Son's language—but when I am dishonest, when I mislead others in any way, I am speaking the language of my enemy.

LIVE HONESTLY

Live in the fear of GOD—be most careful,
for GOD hates dishonesty, partiality, and bribery.

2 CHRONICLES 19:7 MSG

Human nature is predictable: it always seeks comfort, pleasure, and plenty, and it avoids difficulty, pain, and loss. That is why people are so often tempted to cut corners at work or to fudge numbers when charging customers or paying taxes. Sometimes it seems that dishonesty is the default setting of mankind.

Partiality is another way of bending the rules. While you may be convinced that you treat everyone the same, do you show favorites by allowing certain people privileges, access, and leniency that you don't offer to others?

And while you might be dismayed at the blatant bribery in Third World countries, it is nevertheless alive (in its more polite forms) in our own country. For example, are you more inclined to do things promptly and well for people who have shown favors to you or scratched your back in some way?

The best way to avoid dishonesty and partiality is to revere God and seek to please Him. Then He will help you to be honest in all your dealings with others.

HONESTY AND DISHONESTY

Honesty guides good people; dishonesty
destroys treacherous people.
PROVERBS 11:3 NLT

Picture yourself traveling through unfamiliar territory in the dark. The path has many forks, and you have no idea which way to choose. Would you be happy if someone who knows that region like the back of his hand offered to guide you to your destination? Of course!

Life itself is often dark, unfamiliar territory. But you can know that you are walking on the right path if you have honesty guiding your steps.

Many times, if you choose what is honest, you seem to be losing out—while unscrupulous, crooked people who take devious shortcuts get ahead in life. But you avoid many pitfalls by having integrity. For one thing, if you both get audited, he is the one who suffers.

And if you consistently own up to your mistakes instead of trying to wiggle out of any responsibility, you will gain a reputation for honesty. This will serve you well.

It may take a while, sometimes years, but dishonesty eventually destroys those foolish enough to indulge in it. "Better to be poor and honest than to be dishonest and a fool" (Proverbs 19:1 NLT).

PRINCIPLES OF HONESTY

Whoever is dishonest with very little
will also be dishonest with much.

LUKE 16:10 NIV

How you handle dimes and dollars is a very good indicator of how you will handle a much larger amount. You might think that small sums of money aren't significant—it is all slush fund until it reaches a certain threshold. But God watches how honest you are with pocket change before He trusts you with more.

The aggregate effect of small, corrupt money habits carries a huge price tag. Even a small hole will eventually sink a large ship. The continual dripping of a leaky faucet will, over time, drain your tank dry. And as Solomon put it, "the little foxes. . .ruin the vineyards" (Song of Songs 2:15 NIV).

Besides, if you are used to spending money recklessly and aren't on the level with small sums, your habits will continue unchanged if you come into a large amount of money. You will be even more likely to fudge on your tax forms with big sums of money.

Determine to be scrupulously honest. Doing so may require a constant focus for some time, but eventually you will form new habits.

ENTIRELY HONEST

*They must not. . .steal, but must show themselves
to be entirely trustworthy and good.*
TITUS 2:9–10 NLT

Many people who wouldn't think of stealing even a piece of candy from a corner store feel no compunction against taking materials or supplies from their workplace. Or they make false statements on their tax forms to save hundreds of dollars.

This attitude seems to have particular appeal if life has dealt them some hard or unfair financial blows. They then reason that they are just "evening things up." Take this one step further and they refuse to speak up if a department store undercharges them $50 for an item. They reason that it is the store's job, not theirs, to catch such things. So much for being too honest to steal a piece of candy.

Often, however, people start off being dishonest with small amounts and progress to being dishonest with larger sums. This is why Christians are to be "*entirely* trustworthy and good" (emphasis added)—honest in that which is least and honest in that which is much.

Make up your mind that you are going to be honest no matter what the temptation before you ever face temptation.

DISHONEST GAIN

*Dishonest money dwindles away, but whoever
gathers money little by little makes it grow.*

PROVERBS 13:11 NIV

What do you do when crooked businesspeople prosper all
around you and never seem to get caught? Meanwhile you
work hard, operate honestly, but struggle to stay afloat, let
alone get ahead. You can barely sock away enough funds to
pay your taxes, and you often dread Christmas because it is
a yearly reminder of how financially tight you are.

Judgment may not come suddenly on the dishonest, but
their money often slowly bleeds from their bank accounts and
dwindles away. But if you faithfully set a little aside—even if
it isn't much—over time it grows.

Remember, however: this is a financial principle, true
in most situations over time, not an ironclad promise that
invariably comes to pass.

This fact remains: "Better the little that the righteous have
than the wealth of many wicked" (Psalm 37:16 NIV). This is
why James says, "Believers who are poor have something to
boast about, for God has honored them" (James 1:9 NLT).

Distrust

We first learned to trust as babies cared for by loving parents. That most basic level of trust was the foundation on which all our human relationships were built.

But sometimes parents fail to teach their children how to trust. If our parents hurt us, we may not be able to trust others, including God. Or maybe a close friend or a spouse damaged our trust later in life.

God wants to heal our distrust. He knows we can never be whole until we can trust Him. We will never have intimacy—even with God—until we can learn to trust once more.

But You brought me out when I was born. You made me trust when I drank my mother's milk. I was in Your care from birth. Since my mother gave birth to me, You have been my God. Do not be far from me.

PSALM 22:9–11 NLV

God is my salvation; I will trust, and not be afraid: for the Lord Jehovah is my strength and my song; he also is become my salvation.

ISAIAH 12:2 KJV

"Whoever can be trusted with very little can also be trusted with much."

LUKE 16:10 NIV

The hope of the man without God is destroyed. What he trusts in is easy to break, like the home of a spider. The spider trusts in his house, but it falls apart. He holds on to it, but it does not hold.

JOB 8:13–15 NLV

The fear of man brings a snare, but whoever trusts in the Lord shall be safe.

PROVERBS 29:25 NKJV

*Trust in the Lord forever. For the Lord
God is a Rock that lasts forever.*

ISAIAH 26:4 NLV

*And he hath put a new song in my mouth, even praise unto our
God: many shall see it, and fear, and shall trust in the LORD.*

PSALM 40:3 KJV

*"For every breach of trust, whether it is for an ox,
for a donkey, for a sheep, for a cloak, or for any kind
of lost thing, of which one says, 'This is it,' the case
of both parties shall come before God. The one whom
God condemns shall pay double to his neighbor."*

EXODUS 22:9 ESV

*All you Israelites, trust in the LORD—he is their help
and shield. House of Aaron, trust in the LORD—
he is their help and shield. You who fear him, trust
in the LORD—he is their help and shield.*

PSALM 115:9–11 NIV

*Trust in the LORD with all your heart and lean not
on your own understanding; in all your ways submit
to him, and he will make your paths straight.*

PROVERBS 3:5–6 NIV

When they went out, Jehoshaphat stood and said, "Listen to me, O Judah and people of Jerusalem. Trust in the Lord your God, and you will be made strong. Trust in the men who speak for Him, and you will do well."

2 CHRONICLES 20:20 NLV

Our fathers trusted in You; they trusted, and You delivered them. They cried to You, and were delivered; they trusted in You, and were not ashamed.

PSALM 22:4–5 NKJV

"But he who sent me is trustworthy, and what I have heard from him I tell the world."

JOHN 8:26 NIV

And again, "I will put my trust in him." And again, "Behold, I and the children God has given me."

HEBREWS 2:13 ESV

And they that know thy name will put their trust in thee: for thou, LORD, hast not forsaken them that seek thee.

PSALM 9:10 KJV

Consider and answer me, O Lord my God; light up my eyes, lest I sleep the sleep of death, lest my enemy say, "I have prevailed over him," lest my foes rejoice because I am shaken. But I have trusted in your steadfast love; my heart shall rejoice in your salvation. I will sing to the Lord, because he has dealt bountifully with me.

PSALM 13:3–6 ESV

"You are happy when people act and talk in a bad way to you and make it very hard for you and tell bad things and lies about you because you trust in Me."

MATTHEW 5:11 NLV

The Lord is my rock and my fortress and my deliverer; my God, my strength, in whom I will trust; my shield and the horn of my salvation, my stronghold.

PSALM 18:2 NKJV

I want to trust, Lord. But I can't. I want to give You control over my life. But no matter how many times I say the words, I can't follow through on them. I feel stuck. I'm helpless to change. Lord, I know You can do the impossible. Work a miracle in my heart, I pray.

177

CREATING MISTRUST

Don't plot harm against your neighbor,
for those who live nearby trust you.

PROVERBS 3:29 NLT

Keeping your eyes open so that you aren't taken in by every smooth talker is prudent. But some people don't trust anyone and imagine the worst motives in everyone. Suspicion is often mistaken and unwarranted and can sometimes be a thinly disguised hatred for others.

On the other hand, don't betray the trust that others have in you. Don't take advantage of family members' generosity. Don't defraud friends who are compassionate. And don't borrow items and neglect to return them.

Don't even destroy others' trust in you by failing to keep your word, by making excuses to back out of commitments, or by being habitually late for appointments. All these things chip away at relationship and create distrust.

How do you do all this? Simple: love your neighbor. "Love does no harm to a neighbor" (Romans 13:10 NIV). If you distrust and hate your neighbor, you will constantly scheme up ways to make his life more difficult. If you love him, you will be conscious of attitudes and actions that might hurt him and will avoid these things.

BITTER DISBELIEF

Behold, if the LORD would make windows
in heaven, might this thing be?
2 KINGS 7:2 KJV

There is no denying it: Some people have had difficult lives. They didn't have a privileged upbringing and weren't spared this world's harsh realities. They have had to work hard and have frequently suffered misfortune.

Unfortunately, however, sometimes they become cynical. If others have taken advantage of them or defrauded them, they find it very difficult to trust people. And if they attribute their adversities to God, they conclude that He is not worth trusting either.

One time Samaria was besieged for months, and the people suffered famine. When Elisha promised that God would supply abundant food the next day, an official retorted, "If the LORD would make windows in heaven, might this thing be?" He was saying that there was no way this could happen. Even if it looked like it was about to happen, it still wouldn't.

God knows when you have had a tough row to hoe, and He knows a hard life has the potential to make you bitter, but He still asks you to trust Him, to keep your heart tender toward Him through it all.

SUSPICIOUSLY CRITICAL

We're not in charge of how you live out the faith,
looking over your shoulders, suspiciously critical.

2 CORINTHIANS 1:24 MSG

Paul had founded the church in Corinth, and as their father in the Lord, he wrote them "about the authority the Lord gave us for building you up" (2 Corinthians 10:8 NIV). Elsewhere he explained, "Not that we lord it over your faith, but *we work with you* for your joy" (2 Corinthians 1:24 NIV, emphasis added).

When you are first teaching your child how to drive, you might have to grab the steering wheel a few times to avert a major accident. But if they are to learn how to drive on their own, you must take your hands off the steering wheel—and keep them off.

If you distrust someone's motives or doubt their ability to live out their Christian faith, you find yourself wanting to impose detailed rules on them to keep them on "the straight and narrow." This, however, is legalism and doesn't help them to mature in Christ.

How much better to take Paul's approach—to build others up in the faith and work *with* them to help them grow.

Divorce/Separation

When a marriage fails, it hurts. Even if the relationship itself was unhealthy, the final breakup is painful. We are full of disappointment and sorrow. And we may feel embarrassment and resentment alongside our hurt. The future we had hoped for is gone, and we don't know what to hope for in its place.

All we can do is turn to God. In the midst of what seems like one of the biggest failures of our lives, He is there. He has not abandoned us. He still has plans for our lives. And His love for us will never fail.

He said to them, "Because of your hardness of heart Moses allowed you to divorce your wives, but from the beginning it was not so. And I say to you: whoever divorces his wife, except for sexual immorality, and marries another, commits adultery."

MATTHEW 19:8–9 ESV

Now the law came in to increase the trespass, but where sin increased, grace abounded all the more, so that, as sin reigned in death, grace also might reign through righteousness leading to eternal life through Jesus Christ our Lord.

ROMANS 5:20–21 ESV

To the married I give this command (not I, but the Lord): A wife must not separate from her husband. But if she does, she must remain unmarried or else be reconciled to her husband. And a husband must not divorce his wife. To the rest I say this (I, not the Lord): If any brother has a wife who is not a believer and she is willing to live with him, he must not divorce her. . . . But if the unbeliever leaves, let it be so. The brother or the sister is not bound in such circumstances; God has called us to live in peace.

1 CORINTHIANS 7:10–12, 15 NIV

Blessed be God, even the Father of our Lord Jesus Christ,
the Father of mercies, and the God of all comfort; who
comforteth us in all our tribulation, that we may be
able to comfort them which are in any trouble, by the
comfort wherewith we ourselves are comforted of God.
2 CORINTHIANS 1:3–4 KJV

"Fear not, for you will not be ashamed. Do not be troubled,
for you will not be put to shame. You will forget how you were
ashamed when you were young. You will not remember the
sorrow of being without a husband any more. Your Maker
is your husband. His name is the Lord of All. And the One
Who saves you is the Holy One of Israel. He is called the
God of All the earth. For the Lord has called you like a wife
left alone and filled with sorrow, like a wife who married
when young and is left," says your God. "For a short time
I left you, but with much loving-pity I will take you back.
When I was very angry I hid My face from you for a short
time. But with loving-kindness that lasts forever I will have
pity on you," says the Lord Who bought you and saves you.
ISAIAH 54:4–8 NLV

"For the Lord God of Israel says that He hates divorce, for it covers one's garment with violence," says the Lord of hosts. "Therefore take heed to your spirit, that you do not deal treacherously."

MALACHI 2:16 NKJV

To the Lord our God belong mercies and forgivenesses, though we have rebelled against him.

DANIEL 9:9 KJV

The Lord appeared to us in the past, saying: "I have loved you with an everlasting love; I have drawn you with unfailing kindness. I will build you up again, and you. . .will be rebuilt. Again you will take up your timbrels and go out to dance with the joyful."

JEREMIAH 31:3–4 NIV

"The LORD will fight for you;
you need only to be still."

EXODUS 14:14 NIV

*As for you, O LORD, you will not restrain your
mercy from me; your steadfast love and your
faithfulness will ever preserve me!*

PSALM 40:11 ESV

---

*I'm grieving today, Lord—grieving for the loss of
companionship in my life, for the death of hopes, for broken
promises, and for plans that will never be fulfilled. The
pain I feel scares me. I'm afraid I can never recover from
this wound. Give me courage to mourn my marriage. Give
me strength to place it in Your loving hands and leave
it there. Give me hope again. Heal my heart, I pray.*

REJECTED AND DISTRESSED

*"The LORD will call you back as if you were a
wife deserted and distressed in spirit—a wife
who married young, only to be rejected."*
ISAIAH 54:6 NIV

Divorce causes deep pain. If your marriage has ended, you understand this only too well. The emotional pain of such an experience can be excruciating—particularly if you wanted your marriage to continue but your spouse insisted on a divorce. It only compounds the pain if your spouse angrily blamed you for all the "irreconcilable differences."

On your wedding day, you promised to be true, and in return, your loved one promised eternal love and faithfulness to you, and only you. That sacred trust has been broken, and to be rejected afterward in anger and bitterness is devastating.

"The LORD God. . .hates divorce" (Malachi 2:16 NKJV), and He hates it for all the same reasons you do. God feels your pain, and it grieves His heart to see you go through such emotional anguish. Also, He knows that the breakup of a marriage has other far-reaching repercussions, particularly if children are involved.

Your spouse may have rejected you, but God will *never* reject you.

GOD STILL LOVES YOU

"The fact is, you have had five husbands,
and the man you now have is not your husband."

JOHN 4:18 NIV

Samaritans held to the law of Moses, and one Samaritan woman took advantage of the fact that divorce was permitted to divorce and remarry several times. She eventually ended up just living with a man, something the Law didn't sanction.

Most people in her town shunned her, which is why she came to the well alone in the heat of the day. But Jesus, who spoke clearly against divorce, had compassion on her and had a profound spiritual conversation with her. She very likely decided to legally marry her partner after Jesus' visit, but the point is this: if you have been through a divorce and feel condemned, if you feel like an outcast and a failure, if you wonder if God forgives you, remember Jesus' love and beautiful conversation with the Samaritan woman.

He didn't condemn her. Instead, He led her gently to living water and even used her to bring His truth to her town. God still loves you and longs to speak to you as well.

WHEN LOVE ISN'T THERE

Then she said to him, "How can you say, 'I love you,' when your heart is not with me?"

JUDGES 16:15 NKJV

Sometimes you simply don't feel "in love" anymore. There are things you can do to rejuvenate caring and intimacy, but when you have let things slide for a long time, it takes a complete change of mind and a strong commitment to restore romance. And you may not feel up to it right now.

A temporary separation may be helpful. Paul wrote, "A wife must not separate from her husband. But if she does, she must remain unmarried or else be reconciled to her husband" (1 Corinthians 7:10–11 NIV). At times couples simply need a breather, a little space to think things through.

Often even a separation is unnecessary. When your heart isn't with your spouse anymore, you can't fake the rosy flush of love, but you can show kindness, thoughtfulness, and do small loving acts. And if you are intent on saving your marriage, you will keep at it.

If the other person doesn't respond immediately, don't give up. It can take a while to rekindle emotions of love.

Doubt

Peter was walking along on the surface of the water, his eyes fixed on Jesus, doing just fine. Suddenly, he realized what he was doing. He looked at the waves beneath his feet, and he knew that what he was doing was *impossible*. Instantly, he began to sink.

But Jesus didn't let him. Our Lord grabbed His good friend and saved him. And He does the same for us, over and over, every time we're swamped with doubts and start to sink into life's depths. "Why do you doubt Me?" He asks us. "Have I *ever* let you sink?"

So He said, "Come." And when Peter had come down out of the boat, he walked on the water to go to Jesus. But when he saw that the wind was boisterous, he was afraid; and beginning to sink he cried out, saying, "Lord, save me!" And immediately Jesus stretched out His hand and caught him, and said to him, "O you of little faith, why did you doubt?"

MATTHEW 14:29 –31 NKJV

And have mercy on those who doubt.

JUDE 1:22 ESV

But the wisdom that comes from heaven is first of all pure. Then it gives peace. It is gentle and willing to obey. It is full of loving-kindness and of doing good. It has no doubts and does not pretend to be something it is not.

JAMES 3:17 NLV

But when you ask, you must believe and not doubt, because the one who doubts is like a wave of the sea, blown and tossed by the wind.

JAMES 1:6 NIV

*Abraham did not doubt God's promise. His faith in
God was strong, and he gave thanks to God. He was
sure God was able to do what He had promised.*
ROMANS 4:20–21 NLV

*"Truly, I say to you, whoever says to this mountain,
'Be taken up and thrown into the sea,' and does not
doubt in his heart, but believes that what he says
will come to pass, it will be done for him."*
MARK 11:23 ESV

*The apostles said to the Lord, "Increase our faith!" And
the Lord said, "If you had faith like a grain of mustard
seed, you could say to this mulberry tree, 'Be uprooted
and planted in the sea,' and it would obey you."*
LUKE 17:5–6 ESV

*O Jacob and Israel, why do you say, "My way is hidden
from the Lord. My God does not think about my cause"?
Have you not known? Have you not heard? The God
Who lives forever is the Lord, the One Who made the
ends of the earth. He will not become weak or tired. His
understanding is too great for us to begin to know.*
ISAIAH 40:27–28 NLV

*Take heed, brethren, lest there be in any of you an evil
heart of unbelief, in departing from the living God.
But exhort one another daily, while it is called To day;
lest any of you be hardened through the deceitfulness of
sin. For we are made partakers of Christ, if we hold the
beginning of our confidence stedfast unto the end.*

HEBREWS 3:12–14 KJV

*And when he saw a fig tree in the way, he came to it, and
found nothing thereon, but leaves only, and said unto it,
Let no fruit grow on thee henceforward for ever. And
presently the fig tree withered away. And when the disciples
saw it, they marvelled, saying, How soon is the fig tree
withered away! Jesus answered and said unto them, Verily
I say unto you, If ye have faith, and doubt not, ye shall not
only do this which is done to the fig tree. . . . All things,
whatsoever ye shall ask in prayer, believing, ye shall receive.*

MATTHEW 21:19–22 KJV

Let us hold fast the profession of our faith without wavering; (for he is faithful that promised.)
HEBREWS 10:23 KJV

Arise therefore, and get thee down, and go with them, doubting nothing: for I have sent them.
ACTS 10:20 KJV

Jesus said to them, "Why are you afraid? Why do you have doubts in your hearts? Look at My hands and My feet. See! It is I, Myself! Touch Me and see for yourself."
LUKE 24:38–39 NLV

Jesus, I can't help but identify with Peter—and with Thomas too. I want proof that You will keep Your promises to me, that You are who You say You are, that You will help me to do the things that seem so impossible. Forgive me for doubting.

BREAKING FREE FROM DISBELIEF

"Why do doubts rise in your minds?"

LUKE 24:38 NIV

Some people seem prone to doubting, trapped in a disbelieving mindset. Even Jesus' disciples were often this way. After His resurrection, "He rebuked their unbelief and hardness of heart, because they did not believe" (Mark 16:14 NKJV). Some people, like Thomas, seem especially inclined to being skeptical.

If you realize your faith isn't strong and you don't have confidence that God will answer your prayers, you can take steps to increase your faith. First, you must earnestly desire greater faith and, like the disciples, plead, "Increase our faith" (Luke 17:5 NKJV). God will certainly answer such sincere requests, though it may take a while.

When God begins to increase your faith and you see your prayers being answered, then do all you can to encourage it. Paul wrote to Timothy, "Fan into flame the gift of God, which is in you" (2 Timothy 1:6 NIV). God had given Timothy a spiritual gift, and now that this gift was in Timothy's possession, he needed to stir it up, to fan the burning ember into a fire.

WILLING DISBELIEF

But though he had done so many miracles
before them, yet they believed not on him.
JOHN 12:37 KJV

Jesus was often disappointed that His disciples lacked faith. When they feared during a storm, He asked, "Why are you so afraid? Do you still have no faith?" (Mark 4:40 NIV). He asked again, "Where is your faith?" (Luke 8:25 NIV). He expected them to have more faith.

One time Jesus visited His hometown of Nazareth. Mark 6:2 (NIV) says that the people of Nazareth were "amazed" that Jesus exhibited such miraculous powers. For His part, "He was amazed at their lack of faith" (v. 6 NIV). Their faith was so unreasonably, stubbornly small because they were refusing to believe.

But you can choose to have faith. And when you have difficulty believing, you can pray, "Lord, I believe; help my unbelief!" (Mark 9:24 NKJV). The fact is, you *need* faith if you are to truly trust God and survive the storms of life.

No, you can't work up faith by your own efforts, but having the desire to trust God is an excellent place to start. Cry out to God today to increase your faith.

PLEASING OR DISPLEASING GOD

It's impossible to please God apart from faith.
HEBREWS 11:6 MSG

God loves faith—that is, *real* faith, not constant proclamations of faith when you are actually uncertain. The Bible says that it is impossible to please God if you don't have faith, and to have faith, you must trust Him. To trust Him, you must first come to the realization that God can be trusted.

You may be of a rational mindset. Believing things without evidence doesn't come easy for you. That's not a problem. God doesn't expect you to jettison your brain and leap naively into the dark. He is willing to prove that He can be trusted (John 2:23; 14:29).

The catch is, once He provides proof He expects you to transfer your trust to Him. But many people are unwilling to do so. "Although He had done so many signs before them, they did not believe in Him" (John 12:37 NKJV).

Jesus was willing to provide compelling evidence to doubting Thomas (John 20:26–28). He will do the same for you if you sincerely seek and ask (Matthew 7:7–8). But you must seek the Lord wholeheartedly, sincerely wanting to know the truth.

DOUBTS CREATE INSTABILITY

If ye will not believe, surely ye shall not be established.

ISAIAH 7:9 KJV

God has made many clear promises in the Bible. He has promised that if you love and obey Him, He will protect you, He will provide all your needs, and He will be with you during times of trouble.

You need to do your part, to be sure. But if you do, you can then trust that God will keep His word and do His part. If, however, you feel that He is either unable or unwilling to do so, you have a breakdown in trust and communication. And as Isaiah said, "If ye will not believe, surely ye shall not be established."

You sometimes can't prevent being assailed by a barrage of doubts. Often the devil hurls "fiery darts" to try to shake you from your position and force you to retreat. At such times, you need to raise your shield of faith to deflect them (Ephesians 6:16 NKJV).

Use the faith you do have "that you may be able to withstand in the evil day, and having done all, to stand" (Ephesians 6:13 NKJV). Do this, and you will be established.

Dysfunctional Relationships

It's hard to cope with relationships that are broken. We keep hoping that despite the way things have gone in the past, *this time* things will be different.

We play our own role in these dysfunctional relationships. We may be an enabler, allowing the individuals involved to keep on doing things that hurt. Or we may get sucked into the fights and the hurtful habits.

But God wants to heal our entire lives, including our relationships. This healing is not likely to happen overnight—but our God can do amazing things. A miracle that takes time is still a miracle!

*At my first trial no one helped me. Everyone
left me. . . . But the Lord was with me.*
2 TIMOTHY 4:16–17 NLV

*Love is patient and kind; love does not envy or boast;
it is not arrogant or rude. It does not insist on its own
way; it is not irritable or resentful; it does not rejoice at
wrongdoing, but rejoices with the truth. Love bears all things,
believes all things, hopes all things, endures all things.*
1 CORINTHIANS 13:4–7 ESV

*Therefore comfort each other and edify one
another, just as you also are doing.*
1 THESSALONIANS 5:11 NKJV

*Above all else, guard your heart,
for everything you do flows from it.*
PROVERBS 4:23 NIV

*Then Peter came up and said to him, "Lord, how often
will my brother sin against me, and I forgive him?
As many as seven times?" Jesus said to him, "I do not
say to you seven times, but seventy-seven times."*
MATTHEW 18:21–22 ESV

Then Abram said to Lot, "Let there be no strife between you and me, and between your herdsmen and my herdsmen, for we are kinsmen. Is not the whole land before you? Separate yourself from me. If you take the left hand, then I will go to the right, or if you take the right hand, then I will go to the left." . . . The LORD said to Abram, after Lot had separated from him, "Lift up your eyes and look from the place where you are, northward and southward and eastward and westward, for all the land that you see I will give to you and to your offspring forever."
GENESIS 13:8–9, 14–15 ESV

Where there is strife, there is pride, but wisdom is found in those who take advice.
PROVERBS 13:10 NIV

We have spoken to you who are in the city of Corinth with plain words. Our hearts are wide open. Our hearts are not closed to you. But you have closed your hearts to us. I am speaking to you now as if you were my own children. Open your hearts wide to us!
2 CORINTHIANS 6:11–13 NLV

Live as free people, but do not use your freedom as a cover-up for evil; live as God's slaves. Show proper respect to everyone, love the family of believers, fear God.

1 PETER 2:16–17 NIV

Now may the God of patience and comfort grant you to be like-minded toward one another, according to Christ Jesus.

ROMANS 15:5 NKJV

Do nothing out of selfish ambition or vain conceit. Rather, in humility value others above yourselves, not looking to your own interests but each of you to the interests of the others. In your relationships with one another, have the same mindset as Christ Jesus. . . . Therefore God exalted him to the highest place and gave him the name that is above every name.

PHILIPPIANS 2:3–5, 9 NIV

There was a man sent from God whose name was John. He came as a witness to testify concerning that light, so that through him all might believe. He himself was not the light; he came only as a witness to the light.

JOHN 1:6–8 NIV

He that troubleth his own house shall inherit the wind.
PROVERBS 11:29 KJV

Help each other. Speak day after day to each other while it is still today so your heart will not become hard by being fooled by sin. For we belong to Christ if we keep on trusting Him to the end just as we trusted Him at first.
HEBREWS 3:13–14 NLV

We love him, because he first loved us. If a man say, I love God, and hateth his brother, he is a liar: for he that loveth not his brother whom he hath seen, how can he love God whom he hath not seen? And this commandment have we from him, That he who loveth God love his brother also.
1 JOHN 4:19–21 KJV

Creator God, I focus so often on how I want others to change. I pray for them, I nag them, I lecture them, I beg them, I try to manipulate them. Ultimately, none of it does much good. Instead, God, show me where I need to change. I put myself into Your hands. I'm willing to have You do whatever it takes to heal my relationships.

ROOTS OF SIBLING RIVALRY

When his brothers realized that their father loved him more than them, they grew to hate him—they wouldn't even speak to him.

GENESIS 37:4 MSG

Jacob loved Joseph more than his other sons because he was the son of Jacob's beloved wife Rachel. It's sometimes easy for modern parents as well to favor one child above another—especially if that child is more obedient, attractive, or talented. You may do this without even realizing it. "But if you show favoritism, you sin" (James 2:9 NIV).

While you may not intend to be partial, showing favoritism engenders a sense of entitlement in the favored child and insecurity in the less-favored child. And it sets the stage for a lifetime of sibling rivalries. Many adults trace the roots of dysfunctional family relationships back to childhood influences.

A parent's approval is vitally important to a child's emotional and spiritual well-being. It influences their understanding of God's love and acceptance, views that persist into adulthood. If you have unwittingly contributed to sibling rivalries, you can still make amends now by deliberately, consciously showing love and attention to all your children equally.

RESPONDING TO BULLYING

*Peninnah would taunt Hannah and make fun
of her. . . . Year after year it was the same.*

1 SAMUEL 1:6–7 NLT

Long ago when customs were different, a man named Elkanah
had two wives, Peninnah and Hannah. Peninnah had several
sons, but Hannah was childless. That was hard enough, but to
make matters worse, Peninnah continually taunted Hannah
about it, making her life miserable. This situation went on
for quite some time.

Some bullies aren't fully aware that their words are causing
pain, but others know exactly what they are doing and derive
pleasure from causing others anguish. They enjoy causing
fear by veiled threats. Even if they call themselves believers,
their actions are usually motivated by hatred, and they need
to repent.

If you are a victim of constant taunting, talk to mature
Christians about it. Often, shining light on a bully's behavior
is enough to make that person desist. Even though bullying
is common, people are aware these days that harassment and
uttering threats are illegal.

If reporting the situation doesn't fully resolve it, entrust
your griefs to God. He is able to change things and to bring
peace to you.

OPPOSED BY FAMILY MEMBERS

*"Those closest to you, your own brothers
and cousins, are working against you."*

JEREMIAH 12:6 MSG

The prophet Jeremiah had a tough time of it. He lamented, "Alas, my mother, that you gave me birth, a man with whom the whole land strives and contends! . . . Everyone curses me" (Jeremiah 15:10 NIV).

Jeremiah expected the nation to reject him, but he may have hoped that at least his family would be loyal to him. Nevertheless, even they turned against him. Jesus experienced the same thing. "Even His brothers did not believe in Him" (John 7:5 NKJV).

If you follow the Lord, you can expect opposition. Jesus warned, "A man's enemies will be the members of his own household" (Matthew 10:36 NIV). At the end of the day, this opposition can leave you very discouraged.

Some families are already very divided, even without faith in Jesus being factored in. Brothers and sisters are at each other's throats; people aren't talking to each other and backstab each other. God can change even dysfunctional families. But in the meantime, be aware that they oppose you, and don't leave yourself open to their attacks.

DYSFUNCTIONAL FAMILIES

Son dishonors father, daughter rises against her mother,
daughter-in-law against her mother-in-law.
MICAH 7:6 NKJV

The prophet Micah described a low point in Israel's history. It was a time of unprecedented greed and corruption, and the morals and the structure of society were collapsing. All the judges accepted bribes, and families and communities were breaking apart. Things had become so bad that Micah advised, "Do not trust in a friend" (Micah 7:5 NKJV), and said that "a man's enemies are the men of his own household" (v. 6).

There are many similarities to today, and it is for the same reasons: society is undergoing moral collapse. There is a widespread breakdown in families not only with an unprecedented number of divorces but with divisions within families.

Some families have so much dysfunction and strife that the situation may seem to be hopeless. But in the midst of all this, God's solution remains the same: "Love your neighbor as yourself" (Matthew 22:39 NLT)—and this includes flesh-and-blood family members.

Some deep-rooted grievances and divisions may take time and effort before they disappear, but God's love and power are able to resolve even them.

UNGOVERNABLE CHILDREN

His father had never rebuked him by asking,
"Why do you behave as you do?"

1 KINGS 1:6 NIV

David was Israel's greatest king, a man who loved God wholeheartedly, and God blessed and honored him mightily. "David. . .had not failed to keep any of the LORD's commands all the days of his life—except in the case of Uriah the Hittite" (1 Kings 15:5 NIV).

Some critics, however, insist that David was also a failure as a father, since he never asked his son Adonijah, "Why do you behave as you do?" The behavior in question probably refers to Adonijah thinking that, as oldest son, he should receive the throne. So he "put himself forward" (1 Kings 1:5 NIV; 2:15–17).

Whether David failed or not, many parents do fail to discipline their children, leading them to become spoiled. This creates a dysfunctional relationship. Of course, some teens refuse to be rebuked. The Bible specifically addresses this, reminding children to obey their parents (Ephesians 6:1).

Parents are to discipline their children, but the Bible also points out that some children choose their own willful ways, despite correction (Deuteronomy 21:18–21).

RESOLVING DIVISIONS

*They had such a sharp disagreement
that they parted company.*

ACTS 15:39 NIV

Paul was the inspired apostle who wrote 1 Corinthians 13, the beautiful "love chapter." For his part, Barnabas "was a good man, full of the Holy Spirit" (Acts 11:24 NKJV), constantly encouraging others (v. 23). You would think that they would get along. And for years they did. But one day they had such a heated argument that they could no longer work together.

It began when they were heading out on their second missionary trip. Barnabas wanted to take his cousin Mark, but Paul was set against it since Mark had deserted them previously. Both men were filled with God's Spirit, but they were also strong-willed and opinionated.

Similar scenarios often replay in today's churches and Christian families. Minor disagreements harden into ill will, with both sides unwilling to humble themselves and take the necessary steps to make amends. This can develop into a major family feud.

However, nursing hard feelings isn't God's way. He longs for love, peace, and reconciliation. Fortunately, Paul, Barnabas, and Mark forgave one another and later worked together again (1 Corinthians 9:6; Colossians 4:10).

BLENDED FAMILIES

"You are not going to get any inheritance in our family,"
they said, "because you are the son of another woman."
JUDGES 11:2 NIV

Jephthah's half brothers rejected him because his mother was a prostitute with whom their father had slept. As long as their father was alive, they were obliged to tolerate Jephthah. But as soon as their father died, the brothers kicked Jephthah out of the house, informing him that they had never accepted him as family.

That had to hurt. While such heavy-handed violence is thankfully rare, this kind of rejection is not uncommon. Thank God for blended families who live in harmony, but at times stepsiblings have difficulty accepting one another. Often this is because parents show favoritism to their natural children, and the stepsiblings resent this. Even biological brothers and sisters quarrel and fight, but they may be more inclined to make amends with one another.

If you have God's love in your heart, He will help you overcome such divisions and differences. His Word says, "Sympathize with each other. Love each other as brothers and sisters. Be tenderhearted" (1 Peter 3:8 NLT).

AVOID TROUBLEMAKERS

Here are six things God hates. . .
a troublemaker in the family.
PROVERBS 6:16, 19 MSG

Some people have a permanent negative attitude and try to make others miserable with their constant criticism, quickness to take offense, and continual complaining. Or they spread gossip, creating animosity and suspicion. Perhaps there is someone like that in your extended family.

In Proverbs 6, Solomon lists six things God particularly dislikes, and number seven is "a troublemaker in the family." The New Living Translation has "a person who sows discord in a family." The New International Version has "a person who stirs up conflict." So having a troublemaker in the family was a common problem even back then.

Proverbs 22:10 (NKJV) says, "Cast out the scoffer, and contention will leave; yes, strife. . .will cease." You can't cast an unpleasant person out of the family, but the takeaway here is that you can avoid spending time in that person's company.

If you must invite a family troublemaker to a get-together, be aware of where she is at, and don't take her comments to heart. Let her negativity roll like water off a duck's back. And pray that God will either change her or limit the damage she does.

DOING YOUR FAIR SHARE

"Lord, do You not care that my sister has left me
to serve alone? Therefore tell her to help me."
LUKE 10:40 NKJV

Martha was "worried and troubled about many things" (Luke 10:41 NKJV). Jesus, Israel's Messiah, was visiting, and she wanted to present a splendid feast. They were likely a wealthy family and may have had servants. If so, Martha could have left the cooking and serving to them, but she insisted on micromanaging preparations.

Her sister Mary, however, had chosen to listen to Jesus. After all, Israel's Messiah was visiting, and she wanted to make the most of the opportunity. Jesus commended Mary and refused to send her into the kitchen.

Most modern homes don't have servants, so the right thing to do is to get up and help do the work that needs to be done. If not, one person ends up doing it all—whether cleaning, cooking, dishes, or whatever. And if this becomes a regular pattern, it creates stress in the home.

In a family, every member needs to pull a share of the load. Even children should have regular duties and fulfill them.

FEELING UNAPPRECIATED

"You have made them equal to us who have borne the burden of the work."
MATTHEW 20:12 NIV

When the prodigal son staggered home, filthy and starving, his father threw a feast. His other son complained, "I've stayed here serving you, never giving you one moment of grief, but have you ever thrown a party for me and my friends? Then this son of yours. . .shows up and you go all out with a feast!" (Luke 15:29–30 MSG). It didn't seem fair.

Because the older brother had worked hard every day and tried his best to please his father, he felt unappreciated when his father threw a party for his prodigal brother. Actually, the father was simply celebrating seeing a son whom he had feared dead. Likewise, modern children sometimes misread their parents' motives.

When one of your children is struggling, you may show them extra attention, but although your motives are good, be aware of how things might look to your other children and explain that you deeply appreciate them and all they do.

"We are taking pains to do what is right, not only in the eyes of the Lord but also in the eyes of man" (2 Corinthians 8:21 NIV).

CARING FOR YOUR FAMILY

*Anyone who neglects to care for family
members in need repudiates the faith.*
1 TIMOTHY 5:8 MSG

The Bible says that a strong proof that your faith is genuine is if you love other Christians (John 13:35). It also says that even if you say you love God, you are lying if you hate other believers (1 John 4:20). And you are expected to prove your love in practical ways by sharing food and clothing with them if they are in need (1 John 3:16–18).

It should come as no surprise therefore that God considers love for your immediate family to be definitive proof of your faith. And He expects you to demonstrate love by caring, tangible actions.

Your primary duty as mothers and fathers is to provide food, clothing, and shelter for your children, to meet their medical and dental needs, and to spend time with them, nurturing them. If you are divorced, be faithful with child support. Don't look on it as a burden, but provide cheerfully.

Much needless stress is caused when parents fail to grasp the importance of these basic responsibilities. But obeying this principle is obeying the heart of Jesus' message.

MEETING EXPECTATIONS

Fathers, do not exasperate your children; instead, bring them up in the training and instruction of the Lord.
EPHESIANS 6:4 NIV

Paul instructed fathers not to exasperate their children. Most parents, however, feel that their children's behavior is more likely to exasperate them. You try to train them to do the right things, but they often stubbornly resist, complain, fight with their brothers and sisters, and make you unhappy. This creates ongoing stress in the home and is liable to produce short tempers.

Here is where you have to have faith that a loving approach, constant instruction, and consistent training will eventually have an effect, transform your children from the inside out, and round off their rough edges.

If you lose faith in the gentle approach, you may try sledgehammer tactics, barking out commands and forcing your child to obey. That may well produce immediate outward results, but it won't work in the long run. And it will exasperate your children.

How much better to involve your child in the process! It may take longer for their behavior to change and for them to meet your expectations, but the change will be genuine and lasting.

FRAGMENTED FAMILIES

*All the others care only for themselves and
not for what matters to Jesus Christ.*
PHILIPPIANS 2:21 NLT

For thousands of years, one of the defining traits of a family was that individual members cared for each other, pulled together, and did their share to make things work. The following verse about the church also holds true for a healthy family: "There should be no schism. . .members should have the same care for one another" (1 Corinthians 12:25 NKJV).

Unfortunately, this is not the case in many modern families. Many families are divided and fragmented. Often parents and brothers and sisters live in the same house but "care only for themselves."

Christians proclaim their love and faith in God, but if they focus on what matters to Jesus, then they realize the importance of loving their fellow humans, beginning with their own family members. "He has given us this command: Anyone who loves God must also love their brother and sister" (1 John 4:21 NIV).

Yes, people these days are busy, and they have their own interests. This is understandable. But they need to interact in love and help one another as a family.

Elderly Parents

Our parents' increasing needs seldom come at a time that's convenient for us. Instead, the season of life when we're the busiest with our own families and lives, doing our best to juggle all of life's growing demands, is the very time when our parents are likely to need more of our time and attention.

We may be surprised, though, to find that as our parents age, our changed relationship with them has its rewards as well. Our parents are not too old to offer us love and advice, if we can open our hearts to them. God will bless us through them— sometimes in surprising ways!

Children, obey your parents in the Lord, for this is right. "Honor your father and mother" (this is the first commandment with a promise), "that it may go well with you and that you may live long in the land."
EPHESIANS 6:1–3 ESV

Let them first learn to show godliness to their own household and to make some return to their parents, for this is pleasing in the sight of God.
1 TIMOTHY 5:4 ESV

"Stand up in the presence of the aged, show respect for the elderly and revere your God. I am the LORD."
LEVITICUS 19:32 NIV

Listen to your father, who gave you life, and do not despise your mother when she is old. Buy the truth and do not sell it—wisdom, instruction and insight as well. The father of a righteous child has great joy; a man who fathers a wise son rejoices in him. May your father and mother rejoice; may she who gave you birth be joyful!
PROVERBS 23:22–25 NIV

*Behold, children are a heritage from the L*ORD*, the fruit of the womb a reward. Like arrows in the hand of a warrior are the children of one's youth. Blessed is the man who fills his quiver with them!*

PSALM 127:3–5 ESV

The mother of Jesus and her sister Mary, the wife of Cleophas, were standing near the cross. Mary Magdalene was there also. Jesus saw His mother and the follower whom He loved standing near. He said to His mother, "Woman, look at your son." Then Jesus said to the follower, "Look at your mother." From that time the follower took her to his own house.

JOHN 19:25–27 NLV

"Listen to me, you descendants of Jacob, all the remnant of the people of Israel, you whom I have upheld since your birth, and have carried since you were born. Even to your old age and gray hairs I am he, I am he who will sustain you. I have made you and I will carry you; I will sustain you and I will rescue you."

ISAIAH 46:3–4 NIV

Gray hair is a crown of glory;
it is gained in a righteous life.
PROVERBS 16:31 ESV

Jesus said to Peter the second time, "Simon, son of John,
do you love Me?" He answered Jesus, "Yes, Lord, You know
that I love You." Jesus said to him, "Take care of My sheep."
JOHN 21:16 NLV

Then the women said to Naomi, "Blessed be the LORD,
who has not left you this day without a close relative;
and may his name be famous in Israel! And may he be
to you a restorer of life and a nourisher of your old age."
RUTH 4:14 –15 NKJV

The righteous shall flourish like a palm tree, he shall grow
like a cedar in Lebanon. Those who are planted in the house
of the LORD shall flourish in the courts of our God. They shall
still bear fruit in old age; they shall be fresh and flourishing.
PSALM 92:12 –14 NKJV

Bear one another's burdens,
and so fulfill the law of Christ.
GALATIANS 6:2 NKJV

But if any provide not for his own, and specially
for those of his own house, he hath denied the
faith, and is worse than an infidel.
1 TIMOTHY 5:8 KJV

My son, keep your father's command, and do not forsake the
law of your mother. Bind them continually upon your heart;
tie them around your neck. When you roam, they will lead you;
when you sleep, they will keep you; and when you awake, they
will speak with you. For the commandment is a lamp, and
the law a light; reproofs of instruction are the way of life.
PROVERBS 6:20–23 NKJV

You know how busy I am, Lord. It's hard for me
to sort out the demands on my time. Show me
what my priorities should be. Give me wisdom
to know how to help my parents as they age.

CARING FOR PARENTS

*Their first responsibility is to show godliness at home
and repay their parents by taking care of them.*
1 TIMOTHY 5:4 NLT

For most of human history, people took it for granted that when their parents became elderly, they would take their parents into their homes and look after them. This understanding persists in many countries—and Paul says that such practical demonstrations of love should characterize Christians.

It's good that Christians give to missions or the poor, but "their *first* responsibility is to. . .their parents" (emphasis added). Remember Jesus' reproof to the Pharisees: "You say it is all right for people to say to their parents, 'Sorry, I can't help you. For I have vowed to give to God what I would have given to you.' In this way, you let them disregard their needy parents" (Mark 7:11–12 NLT).

This doesn't mean your parents have to live with you—although it may mean that. They could live in a seniors' home and be perfectly happy and content. But the point is, it is your responsibility to see to it that they *are* receiving adequate care and support. And you certainly should visit them regularly.

A CROWN OF GLORY

The silver-haired head is a crown of glory,
if it is found in the way of righteousness.
PROVERBS 16:31 NKJV

These days it is common for seniors to be great-grandparents and to live well into their eighties and nineties. In Bible times, people were told to respect the elderly. Moses commanded, "You shall rise before the gray headed and honor the presence of an old man" (Leviticus 19:32 NKJV).

When your parents grow old and their hair turns white or silver, they gain a distinguished look. And if they have faithfully served God, the Bible says their hair is "a crown of glory." It's as if they have become royalty. You should respect them even more.

However, as elderly parents' memories begin to fail and their advice comes from a past century, it is easy to ignore what they say. The Bible therefore commands people to show respect by performing such acts as rising to their feet when an elderly person enters a room.

You are to show respect to your parents even when you yourself are an adult.

RESPECTING ELDERLY PARENTS

*Listen to your father, who gave you life, and do
not despise your mother when she is old.*

PROVERBS 23:22 NIV

Respecting your parents is easy when you are a child. They are
the authority figures. But when you become a teen, you tend
to rebel to establish your own identity. As a young adult, you
reengage with them as equals but still respect them, usually
because they are in the prime of life and continue to exhibit
much wisdom.

But making the transition can be difficult when roles
are reversed and your parents depend on you. When they
are elderly, many of your parents' decisions seem naive or
stubborn, and you must patiently explain to them or override
their decisions. Consequently, you may lose a measure of respect for their decision-making ability. This is inevitable, but
don't get to the point that you despise them. Solomon wrote,
"Listen to your father. . .and do not despise your mother."

Don't merely humor your parents. Truly respect them,
even if you must now take the lead in decisions that affect
them. Respecting them means honoring them and treating
them with dignity.

THE BLESSING OF OLD AGE

"Men and women of ripe old age will sit in the streets of Jerusalem, each of them with cane in hand because of their age."
ZECHARIAH 8:4 NIV

In ancient Israel, living a long life was considered a great blessing. However, today many seniors only count it a blessing if they also experience good health to enjoy their golden years. They look in dismay on becoming weak, being housebound, or even needing a cane or walker.

But these restrictions often come with the territory and are part of God's overall blessing of advanced age. Zechariah declares that a sign of God's blessing on Israel was if men and women of advanced age sat along the streets of Jerusalem, every one of them with a cane in hand.

Why were they sitting along the streets? Because they didn't have the energy to run around. So they sat and talked and minded their grandchildren (Zechariah 8:5). Why did all of them need canes? To help them walk. . .slowly.

Your aged parents' weakness need not detract from the blessing of God in their lives.

Enemies

We make enemies out of the people we don't approve of, the people who disagree with what we believe, who have different politics, different values, different agendas. We might deny that we treat them like enemies—but do we act as though we love them? Do we give them our best? Do we pray for them with all our energy?

Jesus tells us that we can't be His mature followers—in fact, we can't even realize our own God-given identities—if we don't start treating everyone, including our enemies, with the same grace and generosity God has shown us.

All my bones will say, "Lord, who is like You? Who saves the weak from those too strong for them? Who saves the poor from those who would rob them?" People come telling lies. . . . They pay me what is bad in return for what is good. My soul is sad. But when they were sick, I put on clothes made from hair. With no pride in my soul, I would not eat. And I prayed with my head on my chest.

PSALM 35:10–13 NLV

For thou hast been a shelter for me,
and a strong tower from the enemy.

PSALM 61:3 KJV

When the LORD takes pleasure in anyone's way,
he causes their enemies to make peace with them.

PROVERBS 16:7 NIV

"But love your enemies, and do good, and lend, expecting nothing in return, and your reward will be great, and you will be sons of the Most High, for he is kind to the ungrateful and the evil. Be merciful, even as your Father is merciful."

LUKE 6:35–36 ESV

Through God we shall do valiantly: for he
it is that shall tread down our enemies.

PSALM 60:12 KJV

[The LORD] freed us from our enemies.
His love endures forever.

PSALM 136:24 NIV

David himself, in the Holy Spirit, declared,
"The Lord said to my Lord, 'Sit at my right hand,
until I put your enemies under your feet.' "

MARK 12:36 ESV

Jesus said, "Father, forgive them, for they
do not know what they are doing."

LUKE 23:34 NIV

For if, when we were enemies, we were reconciled
to God by the death of his Son, much more, being
reconciled, we shall be saved by his life. And not only so,
but we also joy in God through our Lord Jesus Christ,
by whom we have now received the atonement.

ROMANS 5:10–11 KJV

"Have I been glad when a person who hated me was destroyed? Have I been filled with joy when trouble came to him? No, I have not allowed my mouth to sin by asking his life to be cursed."

JOB 31:29–30 NLV

If your enemy is hungry, give him bread to eat, and if he is thirsty, give him water to drink, for you will heap burning coals on his head, and the LORD will reward you.

PROVERBS 25:21–22 ESV

"You have heard that it was said, 'You shall love your neighbor and hate your enemy.' But I say to you, love your enemies, bless those who curse you, do good to those who hate you, and pray for those who spitefully use you and persecute you, that you may be sons of your Father in heaven; for He makes His sun rise on the evil and on the good, and sends rain on the just and on the unjust. For if you love those who love you, what reward have you?"

MATTHEW 5:43–46 NKJV

*Because of his strength will I wait
upon thee: for God is my defence.*
PSALM 59:9 KJV

*Lead me, O LORD, in Your righteousness because of my
enemies; make Your way straight before my face.*
PSALM 5:8 NKJV

*But ye, brethren, be not weary in well doing. And if
any man obey not our word by this epistle, note that
man, and have no company with him, that he may be
ashamed. Yet count him not as an enemy, but admonish
him as a brother. Now the Lord of peace himself give you
peace always by all means. The Lord be with you all.*
2 THESSALONIANS 3:13–16 KJV

---

*Holy Spirit, fill me with Your love. Help me to love
not only You but all those whom You have created.
Teach me not to be so sensitive to slights and insults.
Help me to focus always on what is good for others
rather than myself. Teach me to love as You love.*

BESET BY ENEMIES

Consider my enemies, for they are many;
and they hate me with cruel hatred.

PSALM 25:19 NKJV

Things are often difficult enough already, but sometimes people set themselves up as your enemies and go out of their way to make your life miserable. Paul warned that people would oppose you simply for being a Christian. "Everyone who wants to live a godly life in Christ Jesus will be persecuted" (2 Timothy 3:12 NIV).

Paul added, "Not that the troubles should come as any surprise to you. . . . It's part of our calling" (1 Thessalonians 3:3 MSG). But to expect troubles is one thing—to experience them on an unrelenting basis is quite another.

David prayed for God to consider his enemies because they were wearing him down, and there were many of them. He had practically wandered into a hornets' nest. It was enough to make him throw up his hands and quit.

David said elsewhere, "I had fainted, unless I had believed to see the goodness of the LORD" (Psalm 27:13 KJV). But he did believe the Lord would be good to him. That is why he prayed for God's help.

ATTACKS BY ENEMIES

*My enemies would hound me all day, for there
are many who fight against me, O Most High.*
PSALM 56:2 NKJV

David wrote this complaint when he was fleeing from King Saul and had been arrested by the Philistines. And after he escaped the Philistines, he was back to staying ahead of Saul. David's own people, the Israelites, were betraying him to Saul. He certainly had many fighting against him.

David had done nothing wrong, yet he was on the run like a fugitive. Do you ever feel that way? You try to do what's right but only succeed in angering corrupt people. Instead of being commended for the good you do, you create jealous enemies. Talk about being misunderstood! Jesus also had many enemies, through no fault of His own.

At times in your life you may face strong opposition. Like David, your only hope of surviving will be to focus your thoughts steadfastly on God and cry out to Him. Otherwise you will go under, because nobody can take constant harassment and persecution.

Thank God for times of peace. But be assured that He is also with you during times of trouble.

WHISPERING AGAINST YOU

All my enemies whisper together against
me; they imagine the worst for me.

PSALM 41:7 NIV

Often, your enemies aren't able to do anything to actually hurt you. But that won't stop them from gossiping about you and imagining the worst about you and for you.

When people have decided that you are a bad person, they think all your motives are bad. No matter what you do, they condemn you. You probably wish that such people would get on with their lives and quit trying to wreck yours. But you can't control their attitudes or behavior. You can only control your own.

Ask God to give you peace, and don't worry about them. Keep your heart free of hatred. Jesus said, "Love your enemies, bless them that curse you, do good to them that hate you, and pray for them which despitefully use you, and persecute you" (Matthew 5:44 KJV).

If you love your enemies and ignore the gossip that you hear them saying, "even if they accuse you of doing wrong, they will see your honorable behavior, and they will give honor to God" (1 Peter 2:12 NLT).

GOD WILL DEFEND YOU

*"You must worship only the LORD your God. He is
the one who will rescue you from all your enemies."*

2 KINGS 17:39 NLT

You must spend time in God's presence worshipping Him
and acknowledging that He alone is God. It's not that He
needs you to remind Him of this fact, however. He is already
aware of it. He says, "I am the LORD, and there is none else,
there is no God beside me" (Isaiah 45:5 KJV).

But it is important that you know that God is the only
one true God as well. This is why God says, "Be still, and
know that I am God" (Psalm 46:10 KJV). You need to truly
know that He is the all-powerful God. When you know this,
you have faith to ask Him to protect you.

If you have enemies who are committed to doing you
harm, you need an even more powerful ally who is committed to guarding you from all your enemies. And you have
such a Friend. When your enemies attack, as they sometimes will, God will rise up to rescue you.

You worship God because He is worthy to be worshipped.
But doing so also has powerful benefits.

GOD RESCUES YOU

*You won't be handed over to those men whom you have
good reason to fear. Yes, I'll most certainly save you.*
JEREMIAH 39:17 MSG

Baruch came from an influential family of scribes in Jerusalem, and he served as a scribe for the prophet Jeremiah, writing down his prophecies. But because he helped such an unpopular public figure, he had many powerful enemies.

Baruch was aware that people wanted him dead. But God promised that no matter what political pressures were at work behind the scenes, he wouldn't be handed over to them. God would most certainly defend him.

God has made many, many promises in His Word to protect His people. If He had said these things just once or twice, you couldn't be so certain of His intentions. But He has made it abundantly clear that it is His will to protect you, and He repeatedly tells you not to fear.

At one point, the Jews complained, "The Lord has forsaken me, the Lord has forgotten me," but God replied, "Can a mother forget the baby at her breast. . . ? Though she may forget, I will not forget you!" (Isaiah 49:14–15 NIV).

Facing Death

The closer death comes to us, the harder it may be for us to hold on to our confidence in eternal life. Is there really anything beyond death? Or will all that we are cease to exist once we stop breathing?

The Bible assures us that physical death is not the end. Jesus came to this earth so that our fears could be put to rest. He has promised us that He has prepared a place for us in the life to come—and when we die, we will hear His voice welcoming us into the eternal celebration.

Even if I walk through the valley of the shadow of death,
I will not be afraid of anything, because You are with me.
PSALM 23:4 NLV

So when this corruptible shall have put on incorruption,
and this mortal shall have put on immortality, then
shall be brought to pass the saying that is written,
Death is swallowed up in victory. O death, where
is thy sting? O grave, where is thy victory?
1 CORINTHIANS 15:54–55 KJV

Since the children have flesh and blood, he too shared
in their humanity so that by his death he might break
the power of him who holds the power of death—
that is, the devil—and free those who all their lives
were held in slavery by their fear of death.
HEBREWS 2:14–15 NIV

The life of mortals is like grass, they flourish like a flower
of the field; the wind blows over it and it is gone, and
its place remembers it no more. But from everlasting to
everlasting the LORD's love is with those who fear him.
PSALM 103:15–17 NIV

Jesus said unto her, I am the resurrection, and the life:
he that believeth in me, though he were dead, yet shall he live.
JOHN 11:25 KJV

"I will deliver this people from the power of the grave;
I will redeem them from death. Where, O death, are
your plagues? Where, O grave, is your destruction?"
HOSEA 13:14 NIV

Just as people are destined to die once, and after that to face
judgment, so Christ was sacrificed once to take away the sins
of many; and he will appear a second time, not to bear sin,
but to bring salvation to those who are waiting for him.
HEBREWS 9:27–28 NIV

"Do not be afraid of what you will suffer. . . . Be faithful even
to death. Then I will give you the crown of life. You have ears!
Then listen to what the Spirit says to the churches. The person
who has power and wins will not be hurt by the second death!"
REVELATION 2:10–11 NLV

My flesh and my heart fail; but God is the strength
of my heart and my portion forever.
PSALM 73:26 NKJV

*"For sure, I tell you, if anyone keeps
My Word, that one will never die."*

JOHN 8:51 NLV

*When calamity comes, the wicked are brought down,
but even in death the righteous seek refuge in God.*

PROVERBS 14:32 NIV

*As no one has power over the wind to contain it,
so no one has power over the time of their death.*

ECCLESIASTES 8:8 NIV

*For this is God, our God forever and ever;
He will be our guide even to death.*

PSALM 48:14 NKJV

*And he said, "Jesus, remember me when you come into
your kingdom." And he said to him, "Truly, I say to
you, today you will be with me in paradise."*

LUKE 23:42–43 ESV

*"O LORD, make me know my end and what is the
measure of my days; let me know how fleeting I am!
Behold, you have made my days a few handbreadths,
and my lifetime is as nothing before you. . . . And now,
O Lord, for what do I wait? My hope is in you."*

PSALM 39:4–5, 7 ESV

*(For we walk by faith, not by sight:) We are
confident, I say, and willing rather to be absent
from the body, and to be present with the Lord.*
2 CORINTHIANS 5:7–8 KJV

*We know about it now because of the coming of
Jesus Christ, the One Who saves. He put a stop
to the power of death and brought life that never
dies which is seen through the Good News.*
2 TIMOTHY 1:10 NLV

*Our God is a God of salvation, and to GOD,
the Lord, belong deliverances from death.*
PSALM 68:20 ESV

---

*Jesus, when I read about Your death on the cross, I can
tell You went through much of what I'm experiencing
now. You felt lonely and forsaken. You wondered where
God was. You felt death's pain and horror. And yet in
the midst of all that, You still trusted Your Father. You
put Your spirit in His hands. God, I want to follow Your
Son's example. I commit my spirit into Your hands.*

THE LAND OF NO RETURN

*When a few years are come, then I shall go
the way whence I shall not return.*

JOB 16:22 KJV

When you were young, you probably felt you were nearly immortal. Death, when you even thought about it, was very far off. It was easy to joke about it. But as you get older, you take it more seriously. You finally realize that, yes, you will die one day, and it will be final.

As a Christian, you know that you will go into the presence of the Lord. So death has lost much of its sting. But the best news is that when Jesus returns, your body will be resurrected in great glory and power. In that sense, you do return. But Job was right: you don't return in your weak mortal body once it dies.

You don't need to fear death. Still, dying is a serious matter, and it is understandable that you will feel sorrow at the thought of leaving loved ones and all that is familiar. And regarding your work, you may regret leaving certain tasks unfinished. So even the thought of going to heaven can be bittersweet.

WHAT AWAITS BEYOND?

Then Abraham gave up the ghost, and died in
a good old age, an old man, and full of years.

GENESIS 25:8 KJV

In Abraham's day, people had little knowledge of what awaited after death. They envisioned a vague, shadowy realm called Sheol where ghosts lived in a dim twilight of existence—not really living at all. Was Abraham apprehensive about dying? He might have been.

Yet Abraham was so blessed that the millions of people who died after him were carried by angels into "Abraham's bosom" (Luke 16:22 KJV), a paradise full of light and comfort. Centuries later Moses and Elijah came from this heavenly place and "appeared in glorious splendor" (Luke 9:30 NIV).

This was even before Jesus died on the cross and opened the way to the Father's throne in heaven. We who die now go directly into the presence of Christ. To be absent from the body is to be present with the Lord (2 Corinthians 5:8). For Christians, there is no uncertainty about what awaits after death.

Paul said, "I desire to depart and be with Christ, which is better by far" (Philippians 1:23 NIV).

DYING GRACE

For this God is our God for ever and ever:
he will be our guide even unto death.

PSALM 48:14 KJV

The writer of Psalm 71 was growing older and becoming painfully aware of his frailty and mortality. He implored, "Do not cast me off in the time of old age. . . . When I am old and grayheaded, O God, do not forsake me" (Psalm 71:9, 18 NKJV).

God gives a beautiful response in Isaiah, saying, "Even to your old age and gray hairs I am he, I am he who will sustain you. I have made you and I will carry you" (Isaiah 46:4 NIV). Not only will God be with you when you grow old, but He will be with you right to your dying moment—and beyond! He will literally be your God forever and ever.

He promised, "I will never leave you nor forsake you" (Hebrews 13:5 NKJV). So He is not going to be with you all your life, only to abandon you when you die. The Spirit of Jesus dwells in your heart, and in that day God will claim you as His very own child and take you to heaven.

CARRIED AWAY BY ANGELS

*The beggar died, and was carried by
the angels into Abraham's bosom.*

LUKE 16:22 KJV

When they are about to die, some Christians become radiant with joy and expectation, as if already tinged with the glories of heaven. Some even speak of angels gathering in the room, telling them that it is time to go. So they depart this life with great peace, knowing exactly where they are headed.

Other Christians, while they believe in Jesus, face death with a measure of anxiety and even fear. They don't report seeing angels. So are they not going to paradise?

The answer is that not all people are given a glimpse of the magnificent heavenly dimension before departing this life. Nevertheless, angels come to take all believers home. "And he will send out his angels. . .and they will gather his chosen ones" (Matthew 24:31 NLT).

After describing the sure hope of Jesus returning in the rapture to gather believers to Himself, Paul concludes, "Comfort one another with these words" (1 Thessalonians 4:18 KJV). God's promises give great assurance and comfort that we can trust Him to take us to heaven.

Failure

Theodore Roosevelt once said something along these lines: "The only person who never makes a mistake—who never experiences failure—is the person who never does anything."

Even the great heroes of our Christian faith experienced their share of failure. Abraham and Moses, Elijah and David, Peter and Paul—they all knew what it was like to make serious mistakes. But God used even their failures to bring them to the place where He wanted them to be.

No matter how many times we fail, His love never does. And in the midst of our failures, we can still find victory in Christ.

For we all stumble in many things.

JAMES 3:2 NKJV

But he said to me, "My grace is sufficient for you, for my power is made perfect in weakness." Therefore I will boast all the more gladly of my weaknesses, so that the power of Christ may rest upon me. For the sake of Christ, then, I am content with weaknesses, insults, hardships, persecutions, and calamities. For when I am weak, then I am strong.

2 CORINTHIANS 12:9–10 ESV

"You shall say to them, Thus says the LORD: When men fall, do they not rise again? If one turns away, does he not return? Why then has this people turned away in perpetual backsliding? They hold fast to deceit; they refuse to return."

JEREMIAH 8:4–5 ESV

Humble yourselves before the Lord, and he will lift you up.

JAMES 4:10 NIV

Two are better than one, because they have a good reward for their labor. For if they fall, one will lift up his companion. But woe to him who is alone when he falls, for he has no one to help him up.

ECCLESIASTES 4:9–10 NKJV

If we confess our sins, he is faithful and just to forgive us our sins and to cleanse us from all unrighteousness.

1 JOHN 1:9 ESV

248

*And now why tarriest thou? arise, and be baptized,
and wash away thy sins, calling on the name of the Lord.*

ACTS 22:16 KJV

*The LORD makes firm the steps of the one who
delights in him; though he may stumble, he will not
fall, for the LORD upholds him with his hand.*

PSALM 37:23–24 NIV

*Therefore, if anyone is in Christ, the new creation
has come: The old has gone, the new is here!*

2 CORINTHIANS 5:17 NIV

*"Yours, O LORD, is the greatness and the power and
the glory and the victory and the majesty, for all that
is in the heavens and in the earth is yours. Yours is the
kingdom, O LORD, and you are exalted as head above
all. Both riches and honor come from you, and you rule
over all. In your hand are power and might, and in your
hand it is to make great and to give strength to all."*

1 CHRONICLES 29:11–12 ESV

*For a righteous man may fall seven times and rise
again, but the wicked shall fall by calamity.*

PROVERBS 24:16 NKJV

*Cast your burden on the LORD, and he will sustain you;
he will never permit the righteous to be moved.*

PSALM 55:22 ESV

And we know that all things work together for good to those who love God, to those who are the called according to His purpose. For whom He foreknew, He also predestined to be conformed to the image of His Son, that He might be the firstborn among many brethren.

ROMANS 8:28–29 NKJV

He drew me up from the pit of destruction, out of the miry bog, and set my feet upon a rock, making my steps secure. He put a new song in my mouth, a song of praise to our God.

PSALM 40:2–3 ESV

I do not say that I have received this or have already become perfect. But I keep going on to make that life my own as Christ Jesus made me His own. No, Christian brothers, I do not have that life yet. But I do one thing. I forget everything that is behind me and look forward to that which is ahead of me. My eyes are on the crown.

PHILIPPIANS 3:12–14 NLV

Teach me, Lord, to find You even in the midst of failure. Let me never put off holding out my arms to You so that You can pick me up and put me back on my feet. Thank You that Your grace never fails.

SUCCESS OR FAILURE

They refused to trust him. So he ended their lives in failure.
PSALM 78:32–33 NLT

Worldly people refuse to trust God yet for years may experience "success." However, as their life comes to a close, the glitter of material possessions and accolades fades, leaving them feeling empty. And in the end, they die, taking nothing with them into eternity.

Although the world may have considered them a success, in God's eyes they failed. "For what shall it profit a man, if he shall gain the whole world, and lose his own soul?" (Mark 8:36 KJV).

Even as a Christian, if you focus inordinately on material things and give little priority to spiritual matters, you will end your days in failure. Neglect the Lord and you will experience a sense of futility. You will still be saved but will reach the end of your life having missed much of what the Lord had planned for you.

How much better to make time for reading scripture, praying, and serving God and others, then arrive in heaven to hear Jesus say, "Well done, good and faithful servant. . . . Enter into the joy of your lord" (Matthew 25:21 NKJV).

FEELING LIKE A FAILURE

*"I have labored in vain, I have spent
my strength for nothing and in vain."*
ISAIAH 49:4 NKJV

Some people, as they approach the end of their lives, sigh contentedly that they have no regrets. How different it is for others: they have many regrets! They may feel that most of their life was a failure, especially if they squandered years on alcohol or failed in marriage or as a parent. Or if their biggest accomplishment was to hold down a nine-to-five job and they never did anything outstanding, they may feel as if they accomplished little.

Many Christians could certainly do more for the Lord. However, many people are also too hard on themselves. Even after a lifetime of being faithful to God and their family, they lament, "I have labored in vain." But they can also say with the last part of the verse, "Yet surely my just reward is with the LORD, and my work with my God" (Isaiah 49:4 NKJV).

God sees your faithfulness. You may feel like you have failed, but He says, "I have called him. I will bring him, and he will succeed in his mission" (Isaiah 48:15 NIV).

DOOMED TO FAILURE

"Why are you disobeying the LORD's
command? This will not succeed!"

NUMBERS 14:41 NIV

Disobeying God guarantees failure, if not immediately, then in due time. When you ignore His laws, you set yourself up for a fall. It's the same if you jump off a building: you will suffer the painful consequences, because the law of gravity always works.

In the same way, you can't violate God's spiritual laws and prosper. They too have consequences. After the Israelites refused to go into the Promised Land, God commanded them to wander in the wilderness. *Then* they decided to invade Canaan, but it was too late. God was no longer with them. Moses warned, "This will not succeed!" Sure enough, they suffered a stinging defeat.

Many people live in failure because they refuse to obey God's laws. Even many Christians live defeated lives, spinning their wheels but accomplishing little of lasting value because they are not obeying God.

You can avoid failure by loving God and following His Word. Ask Him to show you what to do every day. Then do it. "Thank God! He gives us victory. . .through our Lord Jesus Christ" (1 Corinthians 15:57 NLT).

FRUIT OF YOUR LABOR

*Strangers will consume your wealth, and someone
else will enjoy the fruit of your labor.*

PROVERBS 5:10 NLT

The Bible commands God's people to avoid sexual sin and
states one of the penalties for breaking this rule: "someone
else will enjoy the fruit of your labor." Yet some people won't
listen, and Solomon describes them later lamenting, "If only
I had not ignored all the warnings! . . . I have come to the
brink of utter ruin" (Proverbs 5:12, 14 NLT).

People also crash and burn through reckless or dishonest
financial practices. If they break those rules, many months or
years of hard work can come crashing down. Failing simply
because things didn't turn out as you'd hoped after doing your
best is one thing. Setting yourself up for failure by cheating
or cutting corners is quite another.

God wants to spare you from failure in *every* area of life.
His desire is to see you rewarded for all your years of hard
work. He wants to see you, not some stranger, enjoy the fruit
of your labor. So stay close to Him and obey Him, and you
will achieve success.

Fear

Fear is a normal and healthy biological reaction that alerts us to danger. Unfortunately, in our lives, fear and danger no longer necessarily go together. Instead, fear can exist all on its own. When that happens, fear becomes destructive and crippling. As Franklin D. Roosevelt said, "The only thing we have to fear is fear itself."

When we find ourselves in bondage to fear, God holds the key that can set us free. When life seems threatening, filled with unknown (and possibly imaginary) dangers, He will be our refuge. He is always there. In Him we can always be secure.

*"But whoever listens to me will dwell secure and
will be at ease, without dread of disaster."*
PROVERBS 1:33 ESV

*"So do not fear, for I am with you; do not
be dismayed, for I am your God."*
ISAIAH 41:10 NIV

*So that we may boldly say, The Lord is my helper,
and I will not fear what man shall do unto me.*
HEBREWS 13:6 KJV

*For God did not give us a spirit of fear. He gave us
a spirit of power and of love and of a good mind.*
2 TIMOTHY 1:7 NLV

*Fear not, little flock; for it is your Father's
good pleasure to give you the kingdom.*
LUKE 12:32 KJV

*"Are not five sparrows sold for two copper coins? And not
one of them is forgotten before God. But the very hairs
of your head are all numbered. Do not fear therefore;
you are of more value than many sparrows."*
LUKE 12:6–7 NKJV

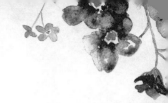

*The fear of man bringeth a snare: but whoso putteth his trust in the L*ORD *shall be safe.*

PROVERBS 29:25 KJV

"And do not fear those who kill the body but cannot kill the soul. But rather fear Him who is able to destroy both soul and body in hell."

MATTHEW 10:28 NKJV

*Fear and trembling come upon me, and horror overwhelms me. And I say, "Oh, that I had wings like a dove! I would fly away and be at rest; yes, I would wander far away; I would lodge in the wilderness; I would hurry to find a shelter from the raging wind and tempest." . . . But I call to God, and the L*ORD *will save me. Evening and morning and at noon I utter my complaint and moan, and he hears my voice.*

PSALM 55:5–8, 16–17 ESV

"Peace I leave with you; my peace I give you. I do not give to you as the world gives. Do not let your hearts be troubled and do not be afraid."

JOHN 14:27 NIV

257

*The Lord is my light and my salvation—
whom shall I fear? The Lord is the stronghold
of my life—of whom shall I be afraid?*

PSALM 27:1 NIV

*I sought the Lord, and He heard me, and
delivered me from all my fears.*

PSALM 34:4 NKJV

*Do not be afraid of sudden terror, nor of trouble from
the wicked when it comes; for the Lord will be your
confidence, and will keep your foot from being caught.*

PROVERBS 3:25–26 NKJV

*When thou liest down, thou shalt not be afraid: yea,
thou shalt lie down, and thy sleep shall be sweet.*

PROVERBS 3:24 KJV

*God is our safe place and our strength. He is always our
help when we are in trouble. So we will not be afraid,
even if the earth is shaken and the mountains fall into
the center of the sea, and even if its waters go wild with
storm and the mountains shake with its action.*

PSALM 46:1–3 NLV

He laid His right hand on me and said, "Do not be afraid. I am the First and the Last. I am the Living One. I was dead, but look, I am alive forever."
REVELATION 1:17–18 NLV

The Spirit you received does not make you slaves, so that you live in fear again; rather, the Spirit you received brought about your adoption to sonship. And by him we cry, "Abba, Father."
ROMANS 8:15 NIV

And it shall come to pass in the day that the LORD shall give thee rest from thy sorrow, and from thy fear, and from the hard bondage wherein thou wast made to serve.
ISAIAH 14:3 KJV

For I, the LORD your God, hold your right hand; it is I who say to you, "Fear not, I am the one who helps you."
ISAIAH 41:13 ESV

Thank You, Jesus, that You have given me Your peace. I know Your peace is not like anything the world has to offer me. Because of You, I will not let my heart be troubled, neither will I let it be afraid (John 14:27).

I SHALL NOT FEAR

Whenever I am afraid, I will trust in You.

PSALM 56:3 NKJV

King David had many enemies and was constantly fighting battles against them. He admitted that he felt fear at times, but he had also learned from experience what to do in such situations. Rather than give in to his fear and run, he cried out to the Lord.

David said to God, "Whenever I am afraid, I will trust in You." You notice that David didn't say, "*If* I am afraid"— as if he was so brave that it was highly unlikely he would experience fear. He said, "*Whenever* I am afraid." He too knew fear. But he knew how to deal with it: he trusted God.

Trusting in God means you believe that God will protect you. This is why David also said, "Though I walk through the valley of the shadow of death, I will fear no evil; for You are with me" (Psalm 23:4 NKJV). Fear is a very common human emotion, and that is why the Bible has so much to say about it and tells us so often how to overcome it.

UNSHAKEN BY BAD NEWS

They do not fear bad news; they confidently
trust the LORD to care for them.

PSALM 112:7 NLT

Psalm 112 opens by saying, "How joyful are those who fear the LORD and delight in obeying his commands" (v. 1 NLT). These are the people whom verse 7 (NLT) refers to, saying, "They do not fear bad news; they confidently trust the LORD to care for them."

King Ahaz, however, is an example of someone who didn't love or trust God. When he heard news that his two worst enemies were conspiring to invade his land, "the hearts of Ahaz and his people were shaken, as the trees of the forest are shaken by the wind" (Isaiah 7:2 NIV).

If you are constantly in the habit of looking to God, it is much easier for you to trust Him when trouble comes. For one thing, if you know you are doing your best to obey Him, you have more assurance that He will answer your prayers. "God does not hear sinners; but if anyone is a worshiper of God and does His will, He hears him" (John 9:31 NKJV).

Confidently trust in God. He is looking out for you.

OVERCOMING FEAR

*"You will live in such fear that the sound of a leaf
driven by the wind will send you fleeing."*

LEVITICUS 26:36 NLT

God warned that if His people disobeyed Him, "I will make their hearts so fearful. . .that the sound of a windblown leaf will put them to flight. They will run. . .and they will fall, even though no one is pursuing them" (Leviticus 26:36 NIV). Today we call this paranoia.

God doesn't desire His children to live in fear, but people bring fear on themselves through disobedience. "God hath not given us the spirit of fear; but of power, and of love, and of a sound mind" (2 Timothy 1:7 KJV).

When you depart from God, your protection vanishes and your fears begin to close in on you. Soon you complain, "The thing which I greatly feared is come upon me" (Job 3:25 KJV). Then you are running from your own shadow—or a scuttling leaf.

If you are plagued by fear, repent of any sin in your heart. Then trust God to forgive you, and He will. He promised in His Word that He would (1 John 1:8–9).

BE OF GOOD COURAGE

Be strong and of a good courage, fear not, nor be afraid of
them: for the L<small>ORD</small> . . . *will not fail thee, nor forsake thee.*
DEUTERONOMY 31:6 KJV

Fear is a tremendously debilitating thing. It can suck the life right out of you. It can make you throw up your hands in defeat before the fight even begins. And if you were in this by yourself, that might be a logical thing to do. After all, why face an enemy who vastly outguns you?

But there is a good reason to have courage: the Lord is on your side. He won't cave in when you need Him most, He won't suddenly realize that He is not strong enough, nor will He abandon you in your crisis. These are very encouraging thoughts.

The enemy will try to overwhelm you with feelings of apprehension, but remind yourself of who is on your side and face down your fear. Don't blink, and even if you are hit with a wave of fear, stand your ground. That wave is merely a tactic of the enemy and will crash harmlessly against the great Rock on which you have taken refuge.

Financial Strain

God uses our financial needs to draw us closer to Him. He hasn't promised that we will be rich, nor does He demand that we be penniless. Instead, He wants us to simply trust Him, whatever our finances. Even in the midst of financial stress, He offers us the prosperity and abundance of His grace. He has promised to meet our every need.

But my God shall supply all your need according to his riches in glory by Christ Jesus.
PHILIPPIANS 4:19 KJV

"For the holy nation of heaven is like a man who was going to a country far away. He called together the servants he owned and gave them his money to use. . . . The servant who had the five pieces of money went out to the stores and traded until he made five more pieces. . . . After a long time the owner of those servants came back. He wanted to know what had been done with his money. The one who had received the five pieces of money worth much came and handed him five pieces more. . . . His owner said to him, 'You have done well. You are a good and faithful servant. You have been faithful over a few things. I will put many things in your care. Come and share my joy.'"
MATTHEW 25:14, 16, 19–21 NLV

Command those who are rich in this present age not to be haughty, nor to trust in uncertain riches but in the living God, who gives us richly all things to enjoy. Let them do good, that they be rich in good works, ready to give, willing to share.
1 TIMOTHY 6:17–18 NKJV

"Do not lay up for yourselves treasures on earth, where moth and rust destroy and where thieves break in and steal, but lay up for yourselves treasures in heaven, where neither moth nor rust destroys and where thieves do not break in and steal. For where your treasure is, there your heart will be also."

MATTHEW 6:19–21 ESV

"Do not keep saying, 'What will we eat?' or, 'What will we drink?' or, 'What will we wear?' The people who do not know God are looking for all these things. Your Father in heaven knows you need all these things. First of all, look for the holy nation of God. Be right with Him. All these other things will be given to you also."

MATTHEW 6:31–33 NLV

What is more, I consider everything a loss because of the surpassing worth of knowing Christ Jesus my Lord, for whose sake I have lost all things. I consider them garbage, that I may gain Christ.

PHILIPPIANS 3:8 NIV

Everyone also to whom God has given wealth and possessions and power to enjoy them, and to accept his lot and rejoice in his toil—this is the gift of God.

ECCLESIASTES 5:19 ESV

Owe no one anything except to love one another.

ROMANS 13:8 NKJV

Praise the Lord! How happy is the man who honors the Lord with fear and finds joy in His Law! . . . Riches and well-being are in his house. And his right-standing with God will last forever.

PSALM 112:1, 3 NLV

Honor the LORD *with your wealth, with the firstfruits of all your crops; then your barns will be filled to overflowing, and your vats will brim over with new wine.*

PROVERBS 3:9–10 NIV

But godliness with contentment is great gain. For we brought nothing into the world, and we can take nothing out of it. But if we have food and clothing, we will be content with that. Those who want to get rich fall into temptation and a trap and into many foolish and harmful desires that plunge people into ruin and destruction. For the love of money is a root of all kinds of evil. Some people, eager for money, have wandered from the faith and pierced themselves with many griefs. But you, man of God, flee from all this, and pursue righteousness, godliness, faith, love, endurance and gentleness. Fight the good fight of the faith. Take hold of. . .eternal life.

1 TIMOTHY 6:6–12 NIV

Teach me, Jesus, to be content in whatever financial situation I find myself. Teach me how to have next to nothing—and how to have more than enough. In any and every financial circumstance, teach me the secret of facing either plenty or hunger, abundance or need. I believe You will supply my every need from Your riches in glory (Philippians 4:11–13, 19).

WAITING FOR ECONOMIC RECOVERY

*"All this misery is from the LORD! Why should
I wait for the LORD any longer?"*

2 KINGS 6:33 NLT

In the days of King Jehoram of Israel, the Syrians had besieged Samaria, and the siege lasted so long that there was a great famine: a donkey's head was sold for eighty shekels ($1,120), and one cup of dove's dung sold for five shekels ($70) (2 Kings 6:25 KJV).

Elisha had been advising the king to trust God, but finally the king snapped, stormed up to Elisha's door, and shouted, "All this misery is from the LORD! Why should I wait for the LORD any longer?"

Your faith can be tested to the limit when you wait and wait for a financial breakthrough, to the point where you are tempted to abandon hope. You may conclude that God is against you and is, in fact, the one causing your problems. So you lash out at those who encourage you to hope. Yet in the Israelites' case, the next day God did a miracle and provided enough food for everyone (see 2 Kings 7:1–16).

God can still do miracles today. Don't abandon hope.

SOARING FOOD COSTS

A loaf of wheat bread or three loaves
of barley will cost a day's pay.
REVELATION 6:6 NLT

During times of war, natural disaster, or drought, the price of food has always risen—and the Bible warns that during the closing chapter of earth's history, prices will rise to astronomical levels.

Food prices have already increased dramatically in recent years. One of the main reasons is that farm machinery consumes much fuel, as do the trucks that transport food. Also, major aquifers that farmers have depended on for decades are running dry. In addition, year after year of no rainfall in major food-producing regions is causing prices to spike.

All of these factors have put a constant financial strain on families, who must now allocate a greater portion of their monthly budget to food.

The short-term solution is to find ways to earn a little extra cash, learn to budget better, and do without nonessentials. But the only solution to the final tribulation and food crisis is for God to bring paradise down to earth, creating justice and plenty for all. As Christians, we earnestly wait for that day.

UNCERTAIN FINANCES

*Take no thought for your life, what ye
shall eat, or what ye shall drink.*

MATTHEW 6:25 KJV

Many Christians consider the phrase "Take no thought for your life" to be impractical advice. How can you help but take constant thought for your life? You need to stay on top of every detail of your work and home life to make sure things get done.

But a more accurate translation is, "Take no *anxious thought* for your life." This is why both the NIV and the NKJV translate this phrase, "Do not worry about your life."

You may have a steady 9-to-5 job that holds no surprises and supplies a guaranteed paycheck. Although you find your work somewhat boring, you don't worry much. But Christ's admonition is especially comforting when you run your own business, are self-employed, or work on commission, and your finances alternate between feast and famine.

And in difficult financial times, with employment more insecure and steadily rising prices, you need the reassurance that God will supply all your needs. He has promised to do just that (see Philippians 4:19). So don't worry.

RUNNING UP DEBT

It's stupid to try to get something for nothing,
or run up huge bills you can never pay.
PROVERBS 17:18 MSG

Contrary to the Bible's warnings, many Christians hope to benefit from monetary windfalls without doing any work. They daydream of winning the lottery and enjoying a life of ease.

It's just as irresponsible to constantly pull out their credit card and run up huge bills with no idea how they will be able to repay them. They may be hoping that God will bless them with huge finances out of left field, but that is not the way God made His world to work.

God's basic financial plan hasn't changed in thousands of years: "Whoever gathers money little by little makes it grow," and "hard work brings a profit, but mere talk leads only to poverty" (Proverbs 13:11; 14:23 NIV).

Of course, when starting up a new business, you often must borrow money to launch out. There are times when you need to take calculated financial risks—with the emphasis on "calculated." You should have a well-thought-out plan on how you will repay the money. Do that, and you will avoid much financial stress.

LOSING YOUR HOME

Even now we go hungry and thirsty. . . .and have no home.
1 CORINTHIANS 4:11 NLT

It's devastating to be uprooted and lose your home. But if you can no longer afford to pay your mortgage, you have no choice but to give up your house. Then you are often forced to move from one cheap rental to another.

Jesus didn't have a home either. After His life's work began, He was constantly on the road. He said, "Foxes have dens to live in, and birds have nests, but the Son of Man has no place even to lay his head" (Matthew 8:20 NLT). He gave up His home to travel around sharing the Gospel.

Paul didn't have a home either. He had "no certain dwellingplace" (1 Corinthians 4:11 KJV). He was constantly moving from place to place, never sure where he would sleep next. But he accepted this and said, "If we have food and clothing, we will be content with that" (1 Timothy 6:8 NIV).

If you are discouraged over losing your house, remember: this world is not your promised home. God is preparing a mansion in heaven for you.

WHEN EVERYTHING IS GONE

*"My husband is dead, and. . . .now his creditor
is coming to take my two boys as his slaves."*
2 KINGS 4:1 NIV

Over a hundred prophets followed Elisha around to learn from him. One of them had a wife and two young boys. They had a small mud-brick house but little else. The prophet apparently became sick and unable to work, so he was forced to borrow money to buy food.

He probably hoped to recover and get back to work, but instead he grew steadily worse and died. The creditor demanded repayment, but since the widow had absolutely nothing, he came to enslave her two sons and work them to pay the debt. But Elisha prayed, and God did a miracle to provide the money she needed.

Bankruptcy wasn't really an option in Old Testament times. People had to pay one way or another. We today can be thankful. Even though bankruptcy is a difficult and humiliating ordeal and recovery can take years, things aren't as harsh as they were in Elisha's day.

If you have had to declare bankruptcy, thank God for seeing you through it.

RICHES TO RAGS

"The Almighty has made life very bitter for me. I went away full, but the LORD has brought me home empty."
RUTH 1:20–21 NLT

During a long drought in Israel, Naomi and her husband, Elimelech, became so desperate that they sold their land to have money for food. When the money ran out, they had to move to Moab in search of employment.

Today both societies and individuals experience financial droughts. You may have gone through a prolonged period of unemployment that drained your savings and forced you to declare bankruptcy.

When this happened, you may have wondered why God decided to make your life bitter. Usually, however, when people go bankrupt, it is not God's doing. Often they are reaping the results of their own financial mismanagement. However, sometimes an entire society goes through a recession. Then many innocent people suffer.

Don't become bitter against God. Trust that He will see you through the crisis. In the meantime, practice what Paul wrote: "I have learned how to be content with whatever I have. I know how to live on almost nothing or with everything" (Philippians 4:11–12 NLT).

EXPERIENCING FINANCIAL RUIN

*Let the creditor seize all that he has, and
let strangers plunder his labor.*
PSALM 109:11 NKJV

Bankruptcy in Bible times was an even more traumatic experience than it is today. When a wicked man was accusing him falsely and fighting against him without just cause, David prayed, "Let the creditor seize all that he has."

This was one of the most devastating things David could have wished on an enemy. A creditor would literally seize *all* that a person had—going so far as to press him and his family into slavery to work off their debt. At least today, if you are forced into bankruptcy, the trustees are supposed to see to it that you are left with enough to live on.

In today's troubled economy, it is not only the wicked and the reckless who experience bankruptcy. Yes, often people end up there due to overspending or financial decisions that, in hindsight, weren't the wisest—but sometimes the innocent are driven into financial ruin by circumstances beyond their control.

God is able to rescue you from the deepest pit you find yourself in and establish your feet on solid ground again.

HOPE AFTER BANKRUPTCY

I will restore to you the years that the locust hath eaten.
JOEL 2:25 KJV

Locusts are a type of winged grasshopper that live, among other places, in the deserts of North Africa. Under certain conditions, they begin to breed abundantly and to migrate. At times they descended on Israel in swarms of 80 billion strong.

They caused unimaginable damage, devouring grain crops and vineyards and even stripping the leaves off trees. Everyone suffered loss and saw the hard work of years wiped out. God said that He sent locusts as punishment but promised that if His people repented, "I will forgive their sin and will heal their land" (2 Chronicles 7:14 NIV).

There is hope of similar healing after bankruptcy. God can likewise restore to you the many years of loss that such an event has wiped out. It will take time, but bankruptcy, hard as it may be, can teach you valuable lessons and a sense of priorities that will serve you well in the future.

If you are going through bankruptcy or recovering from one, take hope. God is in the business of helping people get back on their feet after heavy losses.

Helplessness

We've all heard the expression "God helps those who help themselves." And while there's a certain truth to the saying, the opposite is also true: God helps those who are helpless.

In Jesus' day, the Pharisees didn't see themselves as helpless. They trusted in their own righteousness, in their own abilities to save themselves. But Jesus said, "Blessed are the poor in spirit, for theirs is the kingdom of heaven" (Matthew 5:3 NIV). When we are helpless, when we give up our dependence on our own strength, then God can begin to act in our lives.

I have been crucified with Christ and I no longer live, but Christ lives in me. The life I now live in the body, I live by faith in the Son of God, who loved me and gave himself for me.

GALATIANS 2:20 NIV

We are hard pressed on every side, but not crushed; perplexed, but not in despair; persecuted, but not abandoned; struck down, but not destroyed.

2 CORINTHIANS 4:8–9 NIV

"Then I will ask My Father and He will give you another Helper. He will be with you forever. . . . The Helper is the Holy Spirit. The Father will send Him in My place. He will teach you everything and help you remember everything I have told you."

JOHN 14:16, 26 NLV

In the same way, the Spirit helps us in our weakness. We do not know what we ought to pray for, but the Spirit himself intercedes for us through wordless groans.

ROMANS 8:26 NIV

You see, at just the right time, when we were still powerless, Christ died for the ungodly. Very rarely will anyone die for a righteous person, though for a good person someone might possibly dare to die. But God demonstrates his own love for us in this: While we were still sinners, Christ died for us.

ROMANS 5:6–8 NIV

For his sake I have suffered the loss of all things and count them as rubbish, in order that I may gain Christ and be found in him, not having a righteousness of my own that comes from the law, but that which comes through faith in Christ, the righteousness from God that depends on faith.

PHILIPPIANS 3:8–9 ESV

Arise, LORD! Lift up your hand, O God. Do not forget the helpless. . . . You are the helper of the fatherless.

PSALM 10:12, 14 NIV

Humble yourselves in the sight of the Lord, and he shall lift you up.

JAMES 4:10 KJV

For we do not want you to be unaware, brothers, of the affliction we experienced in Asia. For we were so utterly burdened beyond our strength that we despaired of life itself. Indeed, we felt that we had received the sentence of death. But that was to make us rely not on ourselves but on God who raises the dead. He delivered us from such a deadly peril, and he will deliver us. On him we have set our hope.

2 CORINTHIANS 1:8–10 ESV

"Those who know there is nothing good in themselves are happy, because the holy nation of heaven is theirs."

MATTHEW 5:3 NLV

281

But the righteousness that is by faith says: "Do not say in your heart, 'Who will ascend into heaven?'" (that is, to bring Christ down) "or 'Who will descend into the deep?'" (that is, to bring Christ up from the dead). But what does it say? "The word is near you; it is in your mouth and in your heart."

ROMANS 10:6–8 NIV

If I must boast, I will boast of the things that show my weakness.

2 CORINTHIANS 11:30 NIV

An argument arose among them as to which of them was the greatest. But Jesus, knowing the reasoning of their hearts, took a child and put him by his side and said to them, "Whoever receives this child in my name receives me, and whoever receives me receives him who sent me. For he who is least among you all is the one who is great."

LUKE 9:46–48 ESV

God, give me a healthy humility that depends on Your strength as my help and refuge. May my sense of helplessness not be based on lies I tell myself, however. When I hear myself saying things like, "There's no way I can get out of this mess," or "Life hasn't been fair to me, so why should I even try anymore?" remind me that these words are not the truth. Give me the courage that's based on confidence in Your strength.

YOU ARE NOT HELPLESS

I can do everything through Christ, who gives me strength.
PHILIPPIANS 4:13 NLT

At times you will be overwhelmed by problems and circumstances, and it can be frightening to be swept along by situations that seem to be completely beyond your control.

But although you are powerless to deal with insurmountable problems, you are never completely helpless, because the all-powerful God is with you. Christ lives in you, and He can strengthen you and give you solutions and just the right answers.

The armies of Israel felt helpless against Goliath, but David, emboldened by the Spirit of God, faced the giant and defeated him. Paul tells us, "Be strong in the Lord, and in the power of his might" (Ephesians 6:10 KJV).

Do you feel weak and helpless? Rejoice! This gives God the opportunity to work miracles through you. As Paul wrote, "When I am weak, then am I strong" (2 Corinthians 12:10 KJV). God assured him, "My strength is made perfect in weakness" (2 Corinthians 12:9 KJV).

Even when things are darkest, you can always pray. God can do the impossible, and with Him on your side, things are never completely out of control.

THE HOPES OF THE HELPLESS

*Lord, you know the hopes of the helpless. Surely
you will hear their cries and comfort them.*

PSALM 10:17 NLT

Many people today are helpless. They are boxed into desperate situations over which they have no control. Their only recourse is to cry out to God.

This applies to families trying to make ends meet on a limited budget—only to be hit by a large, unexpected expense. It applies to single mothers trying to raise children in a difficult part of town. It applies to seniors struggling with health issues. God knows each of their sorrows and needs, and He hears their cries for help.

Usually, however, God doesn't do outstanding miracles and completely transform their situations. Instead, He answers incrementally, day by day, in almost imperceptible ways, helping them manage through desperate times and comforting them in their sorrow. "Blessed be God. . .the Father of mercies, and the God of all comfort" (2 Corinthians 1:3 KJV).

God knows the hopes of the helpless, His heart is moved by their pain, and He acts to bring them relief, even when it seems that He is not present.

UTTERLY HELPLESS

I am utterly helpless, without any chance of success.
JOB 6:13 NLT

After losing all his earthly belongings—and even his family—in a series of calamities, and after months of suffering painful boils all over his body, Job was ready to call it quits. He lamented, "I have nothing to live for" (Job 6:11 NLT). He had been completely beaten down.

Job was convinced that no matter what he attempted, he would fail. He had absolutely zero chance of succeeding in anything he tried to do. So why even bother?

Sometimes you may feel that way. Life has dealt you hard blows, and just when you are struggling to get back on your feet, you are knocked down again. It seems as if God has conspired against you, or even if He hasn't, He still isn't with you while life puts you through the wringer.

But God was always there with Job and had never abandoned him—even if it looked as if He had. God just had to take Job through a particularly difficult season of life, and once that was over, He restored Job's riches and caused him to succeed again. He will do the same for you.

GOD SEES THE HELPLESS

The LORD replies, "I have seen violence done to the helpless."

PSALM 12:5 NLT

Sometimes you wonder if God actually sees how the wicked oppress the helpless—and if He sees, if He cares—because the wicked keep on hurting the weak. But in the verse above (NLT), God goes on to say, "Now I will rise up to rescue them, as they have longed for me to do."

You may be suffering oppression from someone who has great power, and there is nobody to deliver you out of that person's hand. You may wonder how long it will take for the Lord to act.

God often takes His time, but His delays don't mean that He overlooks the wrong that was done, or *is* being done. He doesn't. And though you may be unable to alter the outcome, God is far from helpless. He is all-powerful, and what is more, He is a just God and cares for you. So He will act.

But He doesn't settle every score and right every wrong in this life. Many He reserves for the day of judgment when the righteous will be rewarded and the unjust will be condemned (2 Thessalonians 1:4–10; James 5:1–9).

Hidden Sin

Sin that is hidden still gets in the way of our relationship with God. By hiding it out of sight, we may think we have fooled other people. We may even fool ourselves. We do not fool God.

In the New Testament, Paul makes it clear that our hidden thoughts are just as serious and damaging as our external behaviors. He wants us to be people of integrity and wholeness, without any darkness festering inside us. He knows that ultimately our own selves are hurt the most by these shameful secrets.

*Woe unto them that seek deep to hide their counsel
from the L*ORD*, and their works are in the dark,
and they say, Who seeth us? and who knoweth us?*

ISAIAH 29:15 KJV

*The night is far spent, the day is at hand. Therefore let us cast
off the works of darkness, and let us put on the armor of light.*

ROMANS 13:12 NKJV

*"For nothing is hidden except to be made manifest;
nor is anything secret except to come to light."*

MARK 4:22 ESV

*You have set our iniquities before you, our
secret sins in the light of your presence.*

PSALM 90:8 ESV

*No one who abides in him keeps on sinning; no one who
keeps on sinning has either seen him or known him.*

1 JOHN 3:6 ESV

*Whoever conceals their sins does not prosper, but the
one who confesses and renounces them finds mercy.*

PROVERBS 28:13 NIV

*The sins of some men can be seen. Their sins go before them and
make them guilty. The sins of other men will be seen later.*

1 TIMOTHY 5:24 NLV

*No one can hide from God. His eyes see everything we do.
We must give an answer to God for what we have done.
We have a great Religious Leader Who has made the way
for man to go to God. He is Jesus, the Son of God, Who has
gone to heaven to be with God. Let us keep our trust in
Jesus Christ. Our Religious Leader understands how weak
we are. Christ was tempted in every way we are tempted,
but He did not sin. Let us go with complete trust to the
throne of God. We will receive His loving-kindness and
have His loving-favor to help us whenever we need it.*

HEBREWS 4:13–16 NLV

*"My eyes are on all their ways; they are not hidden
from me, nor is their sin concealed from my eyes."*

JEREMIAH 16:17 NIV

And they heard the sound of the Lord *God walking in the
garden in the cool of the day, and the man and his wife hid
themselves from the presence of the* Lord *God among the trees
of the garden. But the* Lord *God called to the man and said to
him, "Where are you?" And he said, "I heard the sound of you
in the garden, and I was afraid, because I was naked, and I hid
myself." He said, "Who told you that you were naked? Have
you eaten of the tree of which I commanded you not to eat?"*

GENESIS 3:8–11 ESV

If we claim to be without sin, we deceive ourselves and the truth is not in us. If we confess our sins, he is faithful and just and will forgive us our sins and purify us from all unrighteousness.

1 JOHN 1:8–9 NIV

When I kept silent, my bones grew old through my groaning all the day long. For day and night Your hand was heavy upon me; my vitality was turned into the drought of summer. I acknowledged my sin to You, and my iniquity I have not hidden. I said, "I will confess my transgressions to the LORD," and You forgave the iniquity of my sin.

PSALM 32:3–5 NKJV

"Have I hidden my sins like Adam? Have I hidden my wrong-doing in my heart. . . . If only I had one to hear me! See, here my name is written. Let the All-powerful answer me! May what is against me be written down! For sure I would carry it on my shoulder. I would tie it around my head like a crown. I would tell Him the number of my every step. I would come near Him like a prince."

JOB 31:33, 35–37 NLV

Teach me, Lord, never to be dishonest with myself or You. Examine my heart, and reveal its contents. May there be no secrets between us.

GOD SEARCHES YOUR HEART

Search me, O God, and know my heart: try me, and know
my thoughts: and see if there be any wicked way in me.
PSALM 139:23–24 KJV

All Christians sin from time to time. But God is more than willing to forgive. "If we say that we have no sin, we deceive ourselves. . . . If we confess our sins, he is faithful and just to forgive us our sins, and to cleanse us from all unrighteousness" (1 John 1:8–9 KJV).

However, the problem comes when believers don't seek to make things right. Sometimes you don't recognize that you have done wrong, or—as is often the case—you are aware that you have sinned but aren't ready to repent. Or you don't take your sin seriously. You tell yourself that you are only human, and it is a trifling matter, after all.

But sin causes a disconnect in your relationship with God, so it is wise to pray, "Search me, O God," and then listen carefully to what He brings to your attention. If you want to walk in the light, you must continually surrender any darkness in your life to God.

COVERING SIN

*He who covers his sins will not prosper, but whoever
confesses and forsakes them will have mercy.*

PROVERBS 28:13 NKJV

Sometimes believers struggle with hidden sin. They are in agony over something they have done but are scared to bring it to the light. The reason is shame or fear: they worry about their reputations. What would people think if they knew they had done such a selfish thing? No, they reason, better to keep it covered. So they continue to suffer—and to miss out on the blessings God longs to give them—because "he who covers his sins will not prosper."

There is wisdom in not describing a private sin (something that concerns only the sinner and God) publicly. Since so many people love gossip, the sinner would only open himself to needless pain. Also, if he has offended someone, the Bible says that the ideal solution is to go to that person alone and apologize (Matthew 18:15).

Confessing certain personal faults to mature spiritual friends is also appropriate at times. "Confess your faults one to another, and pray one for another, that ye may be healed" (James 5:16 KJV). God longs to give you both wisdom and peace.

Hopelessness

We tend to think of hope as a cheery, optimistic outlook on life. But the biblical concept of hope is far greater and deeper. It is a confidence and expectation in what God will do in the future, an understanding that the same God who was with us yesterday will be with us tomorrow.

When things seem hopeless, we are robbed of this confidence. We feel as though the future is empty and barren. But hopelessness is always a lie, for our God has big plans for us! No matter how hard the road, it always leads us into His presence.

Our hope comes from God. May He fill you with joy and peace because of your trust in Him. May your hope grow stronger by the power of the Holy Spirit.
ROMANS 15:13 NLV

For God alone, O my soul, wait in silence, for my hope is from him.
PSALM 62:5 ESV

Be joyful in hope, patient in affliction, faithful in prayer.
ROMANS 12:12 NIV

Blessed be the God and Father of our Lord Jesus Christ, who according to His abundant mercy has begotten us again to a living hope through the resurrection of Jesus Christ from the dead, to an inheritance incorruptible and undefiled and that does not fade away, reserved in heaven for you, who are kept by the power of God through faith for salvation ready to be revealed in the last time. In this you greatly rejoice, though now for a little while, if need be, you have been grieved by various trials, that the genuineness of your faith, being much more precious than gold that perishes, though it is tested by fire, may be found to praise, honor, and glory at the revelation of Jesus Christ.
1 PETER 1:3–7 NKJV

Thou art my hiding place and my shield: I hope in thy word.
PSALM 119:114 KJV

"For I know the plans I have for you," says the Lord, "plans for well-being and not for trouble, to give you a future and a hope."
JEREMIAH 29:11 NLV

Life will be brighter than noonday, and darkness will become like morning. You will be secure, because there is hope.
JOB 11:17–18 NIV

"You wearied yourself by such going about, but you would not say, 'It is hopeless.' You found renewal of your strength, and so you did not faint."
ISAIAH 57:10 NIV

"For there is hope for a tree, if it is cut down, that it will sprout again, and that its tender shoots will not cease."
JOB 14:7 NKJV

We rejoice in our sufferings, knowing that suffering produces endurance, and endurance produces character, and character produces hope, and hope does not put us to shame, because God's love has been poured into our hearts through the Holy Spirit who has been given to us.
ROMANS 5:3–5 ESV

In hope he believed against hope, that he should become the father of many nations, as he had been told, "So shall your offspring be."
ROMANS 4:18 ESV

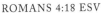

Why art thou cast down, O my soul? and why art thou disquieted in me? hope thou in God: for I shall yet praise him for the help of his countenance.

PSALM 42:5 KJV

Everything that has been made in the world is weak. It is not that the world wanted it to be that way. God allowed it to be that way. Yet there is hope.

ROMANS 8:20 NLV

If in Christ we have hope in this life only, we are of all people most to be pitied. But in fact Christ has been raised from the dead, the firstfruits of those who have fallen asleep. For as by a man came death, by a man has come also the resurrection of the dead. For as in Adam all die, so also in Christ shall all be made alive.

1 CORINTHIANS 15:19–22 ESV

Now may our Lord Jesus Christ himself, and God our Father, who loved us and gave us eternal comfort and good hope through grace, comfort your hearts and establish them in every good work and word.

2 THESSALONIANS 2:16–17 ESV

Jesus, You promised never to leave me or forsake me. Because of You, I have hope. I know this hope will never be put to shame.

GOD NEVER DISREGARDS YOU

Why do you complain, Jacob? Why do you say,
Israel, "My way is hidden from the LORD;
my cause is disregarded by my God"?

ISAIAH 40:27 NIV

Hope, along with love and faith, is a key virtue (1 Corinthians 13:13). To lose hope leaves a great gnawing emptiness inside you. Though you still believe in God, if you lose hope that He loves you and think that He has turned His face away, you are basically just a shell of yourself.

Imagine being convinced that God cares so little about you that He completely ignores you. He is aware that you are mired in problems, but He simply can't be bothered to help you or comfort you. Talk about hopelessness!

The truth is very different. God loves you, and your cause is constantly before His eyes. He made certain of that by permanently etching your name on His hands. He says, "Can a mother forget the baby at her breast. . . ? Though she may forget, I will not forget you! See, I have engraved you on the palms of my hands" (Isaiah 49:15–16 NIV).

God sees what you are going through, and He cares immensely.

WITHSTANDING FEAR

"We're all afraid. Everyone in the country feels hopeless."
JOSHUA 2:9 MSG

When God was ready to lead the Israelites into Canaan, He struck great fear into the hearts of the Canaanites so they'd melt away before His people. The Lord did amazing miracles to convince them that it was futile to fight Him. And it worked. The harlot Rahab told the spies, "We're all afraid. Everyone in the country feels hopeless."

However, sometimes God's people experience paralyzing fear too. This often happens when they are disobeying Him in some way. God warned, "There were they in great fear, where no fear was" (Psalm 53:5 KJV). Many people today are afraid even when they are not in imminent danger. The solution is to get their hearts right with God as quickly as possible. Then the fears and delusions will melt away.

Or the problem might not be sin; perhaps they succumb to fear and think their situation is hopeless because they are not spending enough time in prayer, looking to God. Remember the Bible's promise: "You will keep him in perfect peace, whose mind is stayed on You, because he trusts in You" (Isaiah 26:3 NKJV).

HOPELESSLY CONFUSED

Live no longer as the Gentiles do,
for they are hopelessly confused.
EPHESIANS 4:17 NLT

Before you were saved, "you were separate from Christ. . . without hope and without God in the world" (Ephesians 2:12 NIV). You were lost and condemned. You had no purpose for living. The Bible describes this, saying: "Our days on earth are like a shadow, without hope" (1 Chronicles 29:15 NIV).

But when Jesus saved you, you gained "hope as an anchor for the soul, firm and secure" (Hebrews 6:19 NIV). This renewed your way of thinking and gave you tremendous peace and joy.

But it is important to grow in your faith and to continue to forsake your old life, such as the world's take on sexual morality or its views on spiritual truth. If you fail to do this and continue to buy into the world's philosophies, their influence will grow like yeast in a lump of dough (Galatians 5:8–9) until you eventually become confused again.

That is why the Bible commands, "Stand fast therefore in the liberty by which Christ has made us free, and do not be entangled again with a yoke of bondage" (Galatians 5:1 NKJV).

WHAT'S THE USE?

*"The verdict has already been handed down—
'Guilty!'—so what's the use of protests or appeals?"*

JOB 9:28 MSG

Sometimes you may feel like Job: there is no use in complaining to God about your situation. He has already decided to punish you, and nothing you can say or do will change things. Usually this kind of hopelessness pervades your spirit when you have sinned and aren't sure if God has forgiven you.

Or it could come over you if God is convicting you about some fault or some wrong for which you have never apologized, and you are unwilling to give up the habit or to make things right. Your own heart condemns you. After a while you may even forget why God is bearing down on you—and you just have a general feeling of hopelessness hanging like a cloud over your head.

Pray today and ask God to work in your heart and bring you to repentance. "If we confess our sins, He is faithful and just to forgive us our sins and to cleanse us from all unrighteousness" (1 John 1:9 NKJV). Then believe that He *has* forgiven you and move on.

BELIEVING FOR THE IMPOSSIBLE

"All this may seem impossible to you now. . . .
But is it impossible for me?"

ZECHARIAH 8:6 NLT

A handful of Jews had returned from captivity to Judah, but it was a long, hard journey, and few elderly people or children had come. But God promised that the streets of Jerusalem would be full of boys and girls at play and aged men and women sitting. This population explosion seemed impossible, but God said it would happen.

Sometimes God asks you, too, to believe the impossible. He realizes that to your limited knowledge the situation may seem hopeless, but He seeks to remind you that He is the all-powerful Creator of the heavens and the earth, and that nothing is impossible for Him.

Perhaps you have no problem with that but just don't believe that God cares enough about your circumstances to do the miracle. To this He says, "For I know the plans I have for you. . .plans to prosper you and not to harm you, plans to give you hope and a future" (Jeremiah 29:11 NIV).

With God on your side, your situation is far from hopeless.

Infertility

When you can't become pregnant, you may feel as though you are unworthy, worthless. Even in this day of women's rights, you may still believe that your value, your personhood, your fulfillment all depend on your ability to have a child.

God wants you to beware of this lie. When we become obsessed with wanting something—no matter how good it might be—we turn it into a god. Our value comes from God alone—and we can trust Him to fulfill the deepest longings of our hearts in the way that is best for us.

*For in Him dwells all the fullness of the Godhead
bodily; and you are complete in Him.*
COLOSSIANS 2:9–10 NKJV

And he said unto me, My grace is sufficient for thee.
2 CORINTHIANS 12:9 KJV

*Therefore I say to you, whatever things you ask when you
pray, believe that you receive them, and you will have them.*
MARK 11:24 NKJV

*And Isaac prayed to the Lord for his wife,
because she was barren. And the Lord granted
his prayer, and Rebekah his wife conceived.*
GENESIS 25:21 ESV

*O Lord, all my longing is before you; my sighing is
not hidden from you. . . . But for you, O Lord, do I
wait; it is you, O Lord my God, who will answer.*
PSALM 38:9, 15 ESV

*Your eyes saw me before I was put together. And all the days
of my life were written in Your book before any of them
came to be. Your thoughts are of great worth to me, O God.
How many there are! If I could number them, there would
be more than the sand. When I awake, I am still with You.*
PSALM 139:16–18 NLV

"See, your cousin Elizabeth, as old as she is, is going to give birth to a child. She was not able to have children before, but now she is in her sixth month. For God can do all things."

LUKE 1:36–37 NLV

"Be glad, barren woman, you who never bore a child; shout for joy and cry aloud, you who were never in labor; because more are the children of the desolate woman than of her who has a husband."

GALATIANS 4:27 NIV

Though the fig tree may not blossom, nor fruit be on the vines; though the labor of the olive may fail, and the fields yield no food; though the flock may be cut off from the fold, and there be no herd in the stalls—yet I will rejoice in the LORD, I will joy in the God of my salvation.

HABAKKUK 3:17–18 NKJV

"You will remember all the way the Lord your God led you in the desert these forty years, so you would not have pride, and how He tested you to know what was in your heart."

DEUTERONOMY 8:2 NLV

And by faith even Sarah, who was past childbearing age, was enabled to bear children because she considered him faithful who had made the promise.

HEBREWS 11:11 NIV

*Satisfy us in the morning with your unfailing love,
that we may sing for joy and be glad all our days.
Make us glad for as many days as you have afflicted
us, for as many years as we have seen trouble.*

PSALM 90:14–15 NIV

*For the Lord will not cast off forever, but, though he
cause grief, he will have compassion according to the
abundance of his steadfast love; for he does not afflict
from his heart or grieve the children of men.*

LAMENTATIONS 3:31–33 ESV

*And we know that all things work together
for good to them that love God, to them who
are the called according to his purpose.*

ROMANS 8:28 KJV

*Now unto him that is able to do exceeding abundantly
above all that we ask or think, according to the power that
worketh in us, unto him be glory in the church by Christ
Jesus throughout all ages, world without end. Amen.*

EPHESIANS 3:20–21 KJV

---

*Lord, I'm trying to accept whatever You want for
my life. But it's so hard. You know how much I long
for a child. Help me to give this longing to You.*

DESPERATE FOR CHILDREN

*When Rachel saw that she wasn't having any children. . . .
she pleaded with Jacob, "Give me children, or I'll die!"*

GENESIS 30:1 NLT

God put a natural desire in most women to have babies. They may go for years enjoying the carefree single life, with little desire to have children. Then the nesting instinct kicks in with a vengeance and they simply *must* have children to feel complete. God designed things this way to ensure that the human race continues.

This is why Bible women who weren't able to bear children went through such tremendous trials. We see this with Sarah, and with Hannah and Elizabeth. But no woman illustrates this better than Rachel. After she had gone years without conceiving, she became so desperate that she literally felt like dying.

Many women today also struggle with infertility. Although they have tried to get pregnant and have undergone extensive fertility treatments, nothing seems to work. And attempts at adoption face major roadblocks.

But God has done miracles in the past, and He is still able today. Don't give up hope. One way or another, God can see to it that you have children.

CONTENT IN GOD

Whom have I in heaven but You? And there is none upon earth that I desire besides You.

PSALM 73:25 NKJV

It's a natural, good thing for a woman to desire to become pregnant—even to long earnestly for a child and to pray fervently for one. But there is a danger even in desiring good things: if you become so obsessed with something that you can't be happy without it, you have exalted your desire above God.

In addition, God intends that you find your ultimate fulfillment in Him. You aren't born with this desire. It has to be *learned*. Paul said, "I have learned to be content whatever the circumstances" (Philippians 4:11 NIV).

Often Christians claim the promise: "Delight yourself also in the LORD, and He shall give you the desires of your heart" (Psalm 37:4 NKJV). They reason, "I love God, so He is obligated to give me whatever I want." But delighting yourself in the Lord means choosing God's will, *whatever* it is, even if it runs contrary to your desires. And it sometimes does.

Certainly you should present your petitions to God. But then rest them at His feet and submit to Him.

Insomnia

Insomnia makes us tired and cranky. When we're tired, we're more likely to feel anxious or depressed. It becomes a vicious cycle: the more upset and tense we become, the less we can sleep; the less we sleep, the more upset and tense we become. . . .

We may end up afraid to even go to bed because we don't want to face the frustration we feel when we lie there awake again. Anxiety overwhelms us. We feel helpless.

But God is with us, even when we lie awake night after night. He has compassion on our sleeplessness. His love never fails.

Take my yoke upon you, and learn of me; for I am meek and lowly in heart: and ye shall find rest unto your souls.

MATTHEW 11:29 KJV

Truly my soul finds rest in God. . . .
Yes, my soul, find rest in God.

PSALM 62:1, 5 NIV

He gives His beloved sleep.

PSALM 127:2 NKJV

In peace I will both lie down and sleep; for you alone, O LORD, make me dwell in safety.

PSALM 4:8 ESV

Dear children, keep yourselves from idols.

1 JOHN 5:21 NIV

My God, I cry out by day, but you do not answer, by night, but I find no rest. Yet you are enthroned as the Holy One; you are the one Israel praises. In you our ancestors put their trust; they trusted and you delivered them. To you they cried out and were saved; in you they trusted and were not put to shame.

PSALM 22:2–5 NIV

*Whoever dwells in the shelter of the Most High
will rest in the shadow of the Almighty.*
PSALM 91:1 NIV

*Return to your rest, O my soul. For the
Lord has been good to you.*
PSALM 116:7 NLV

*One day he got into a boat with his disciples, and he said to
them, "Let us go across to the other side of the lake." So they
set out, and as they sailed he fell asleep. And a windstorm
came down on the lake, and they were filling with water
and were in danger. And they went and woke him, saying,
"Master, Master, we are perishing!" And he awoke and
rebuked the wind and the raging waves, and they ceased, and
there was a calm. He said to them, "Where is your faith?"*
LUKE 8:22–25 ESV

*My people will abide in a peaceful habitation,
in secure dwellings, and in quiet resting places.*
ISAIAH 32:18 ESV

Sweet is the sleep of a laborer.
ECCLESIASTES 5:12 ESV

*Therefore I say unto you, What things soever ye desire, when
ye pray, believe that ye receive them, and ye shall have them.*
MARK 11:24 KJV

*When I applied my mind to know wisdom and to observe
the labor that is done on earth—people getting no sleep day
or night—then I saw all that God has done. No one can
comprehend what goes on under the sun. Despite all their
efforts to search it out, no one can discover its meaning. . . .
So I reflected on all this and concluded that the righteous
and the wise and what they do are in God's hands.*
ECCLESIASTES 8:16–17; 9:1 NIV

*Do not worry. Learn to pray about everything. Give thanks
to God as you ask Him for what you need. The peace of God
is much greater than the human mind can understand. This
peace will keep your hearts and minds through Christ Jesus.*
PHILIPPIANS 4:6–7 NLV

*I laid me down and slept; I awaked;
for the LORD sustained me.*
PSALM 3:5 KJV

312

*"You will keep him in perfect peace, whose mind
is stayed on You, because he trusts in You."*

ISAIAH 26:3 NKJV

*Surely I have calmed and quieted my soul, like a weaned child
with his mother; like a weaned child is my soul within me.*

PSALM 131:2 NKJV

*"Come to me, all you who are weary and
burdened, and I will give you rest."*

MATTHEW 11:28 NIV

*On my bed I remember You. I think of You through
the hours of the night. For You have been my help.
And I sing for joy in the shadow of Your wings. My
soul holds on to You. Your right hand holds me up.*

PSALM 63:6–8 NLV

---

*Dearest God, as I lie here in bed, may I feel the echo of Your
Spirit's breath in my own breathing. May the peace of Your
presence lie over me like a blanket. May I recall all the things
You have done for me over the years. Help me to rest.*

SLEEP AND FEAR

*When thou liest down, thou shalt not be afraid: yea,
thou shalt lie down, and thy sleep shall be sweet.*

PROVERBS 3:24 KJV

Worry is one of the biggest hindrances to getting a good night's sleep—especially worry about finances. "The sleep of a laboring man is sweet. . .but the abundance of the rich will not permit him to sleep" (Ecclesiastes 5:12 NKJV). The rich toss and turn, worrying about losing their wealth. They know that all too often "riches. . .make themselves wings; they fly away" (Proverbs 23:5 NKJV).

Of course, many poor people lose sleep over money too. They are not worried about dips in the stock market or a decline in the price of gold. Usually they worry about where they will get the money to pay their bills.

God's promise of sleep applies to everyone—rich and poor. The Scriptures promise, "You will keep him in perfect peace, whose mind is stayed on You" (Isaiah 26:3 NKJV). Stay focused on God's love for you and keep your mind filled with promises from His Word, and He will give you peace and rest. "God gives rest to his loved ones" (Psalm 127:2 NLT).

SLEEPING IN PEACE

*I will both lie down in peace, and sleep; for You
alone, O LORD, make me dwell in safety.*

PSALM 4:8 NKJV

What's your sleep like when you are under pressure, facing stress, or being threatened? You probably have difficulty sleeping. You may hardly be able to rest at all.

When David's son Absalom led an army against him, David fled across the Jordan, where he gathered his own army. David penned a short psalm before the battle, declaring his trust in God. He proclaimed: "I lie down and sleep; I wake again, because the LORD sustains me. I will not fear though tens of thousands assail me on every side" (Psalm 3:5–6 NIV).

Think of the trouble David was in! But trusting that God shielded him and wouldn't allow him to be harmed, he lay down and slept peacefully, without tossing and turning all night. This took great faith. David had to look unswervingly at God, or he would have worried himself sick.

You can't stop troubled thoughts from assailing your mind, but you can resolutely resist them. And as you do, God will give you peace, and you can sleep.

UNABLE TO SLEEP

You don't let me sleep. I am too distressed even to pray!
PSALM 77:4 NLT

Some people, when they wake up in the night and can't get back to sleep, spend time peacefully praying. As soon as they have communed with God for a while, they return to blissful sleep. This isn't the case with other people: they wake up but are too exhausted to properly focus. They *try* to pray but mostly just lay there longing for sleep.

When you are troubled, you are usually highly motivated to cry out to God. Asaph wrote, "When I was in distress, I sought the Lord; at night I stretched out untiring hands" (Psalm 77:2 NIV). Some nights, however, you may be *too* discouraged or troubled to pray. You may think that couldn't be, but it happens.

At times like that, instead of attempting to focus on a long prayer, shoot off short, sincere prayers every time you are able to focus, crying out for help. Quote faith-building verses. Sing hymns or songs of praise in your heart.

God will hear your prayers and answer, and after a while, the discouragement will dispel and sleep will return.

Prodigal Children

Few things hurt as much as watching our children go astray. We long to run after them and bring them home—and yet we must respect their decisions. We ache to protect them the way we did when they were small—but they have gone beyond our protection.

But even when our children were babies, they were never truly ours. They always belonged to God. Only He kept them safe. And none of that has changed. In the midst of what looks to us like chaos and confusion, He is there, leading our children into His peace.

"You in Your mercy have led forth the people whom You have redeemed; You have guided them in Your strength to Your holy habitation."

EXODUS 15:13 NKJV

I am the good shepherd, and know my sheep, and am known of mine. As the Father knoweth me, even so know I the Father: and I lay down my life for the sheep. And other sheep I have, which are not of this fold: them also I must bring, and they shall hear my voice; and there shall be one fold, and one shepherd.

JOHN 10:14–16 KJV

Rejoice always, pray without ceasing, in everything give thanks; for this is the will of God in Christ Jesus for you.

1 THESSALONIANS 5:16–18 NKJV

And we know that all things work together for good to those who love God, to those who are the called according to His purpose.

ROMANS 8:28 NKJV

"For my thoughts are not your thoughts, neither are your ways my ways," declares the LORD. "As the heavens are higher than the earth, so are my ways higher than your ways and my thoughts than your thoughts. As the rain and the snow come down from heaven, and do not return to it without watering the earth and making it bud and flourish, so that it yields seed for the sower and bread for the eater, so is my word that goes out from my mouth: It will not return to me empty, but will accomplish what I desire and achieve the purpose for which I sent it."

ISAIAH 55:8–11 NIV

The LORD has appeared of old to me, saying: "Yes, I have loved you with an everlasting love; therefore with lovingkindness I have drawn you."

JEREMIAH 31:3 NKJV

"As a shepherd seeks out his flock on the day he is among his scattered sheep, so will I seek out My sheep and deliver them from all the places where they were scattered on a cloudy and dark day."

EZEKIEL 34:12 NKJV

[Jesus] told them this parable: "What man of you, having a hundred sheep, if he has lost one of them, does not leave the ninety-nine in the open country, and go after the one that is lost. . . . Just so, I tell you, there will be more joy in heaven over one sinner who repents than over ninety-nine righteous persons who need no repentance."

LUKE 15:3–4, 7 ESV

All we like sheep have gone astray; we have turned—every one—to his own way; and the LORD has laid on [Christ] the iniquity of us all.

ISAIAH 53:6 ESV

Christian brothers, if a person is found doing some sin, you who are stronger Christians should lead that one back into the right way.

GALATIANS 6:1 NLV

The Lord is not slow to fulfill his promise as some count slowness, but is patient toward you, not wishing that any should perish, but that all should reach repentance.

2 PETER 3:9 ESV

"So [the prodigal] got up and went to his father. But while he was still a long way off, his father saw him and was filled with compassion for him; he ran to his son, threw his arms around him and kissed him."

LUKE 15:20 NIV

My heart feels broken, Father. I know You understand, for You too must be heartsick when You watch Your children choose paths that lead them toward brokenness and sorrow. Heal my children, I pray, Lord. Lead them in Your paths. I gave them to You when they were small—and now I give them to You again.

WHEN CHILDREN GO ASTRAY

*I have no greater joy than to hear
that my children walk in truth.*
3 JOHN 1:4 NKJV

John wrote that his greatest joy was to know that his children were serving the Lord. And that is true of countless Christian parents today. Seeing your children grow up and claim their faith as their own is immensely rewarding.

On the other hand, many parents live in grief because their children have gone astray despite everything they were taught. When they entered their teen years, they stopped listening to counsel and ceased going to church. And once they became adults, they became fully set in their own way. This is heartbreaking, even if they are not into a wild lifestyle. If they have simply drifted away and show no interest in spiritual things, parents may feel as if they have failed. But the fact is, God has no grandchildren. Every generation must decide for themselves to love and obey God—or not.

The good news is, if parents are faithful to pray for their wayward children, God may yet work in their hearts and bring those children back to Himself.

PRAYING FOR PRODIGALS

*There is hope. . .saith the LORD, that thy children
shall come again to their own border.*

JEREMIAH 31:17 KJV

When the Jews' enemies, the Babylonians, invaded Judah, they took thousands of Jews prisoner to Babylon. Those who had been taken captive wept bitterly. "By the rivers of Babylon we sat and wept" (Psalm 137:1 NIV). And the Jews who had been left in Judah, many of them elderly, grieved for their relatives and children.

Many parents can identify with these emotions. When their children get caught up in lifestyles of partying, alcohol, drugs, and sexual immorality, they too have gone to the land of the enemy. So parents pray "that they may come to their senses and escape the snare of the devil, having been taken captive by him" (2 Timothy 2:26 NKJV).

Even if you pray earnestly with tears, you may have to pray for years, but God hears you. He finally told the Jews of old, "Refrain thy voice from weeping, and thine eyes from tears: for. . .they shall come again from the land of the enemy" (Jeremiah 31:16 KJV). And you can have this same hope today.

PASSIVE REBELLION

"Then the father told the other son, 'You go,'
and he said, 'Yes, sir, I will.' But he didn't go."
MATTHEW 21:30 NLT

Usually when you think of a prodigal, you think of a son or daughter living on his or her own and caught up in a wild lifestyle. But a prodigal can simply be someone whose heart is far from God, even when still living at home.

Jesus described two sons: when their father told one son to go work in the vineyard, he openly refused. The father then told his other son to go, and he replied, "Yes, sir, I will." But he didn't. He had only said yes to get his father off his back. Had he actually gone to the vineyard, he would have done a lazy, careless job.

Many backslidden teens go to church and talk the "God talk," but they are merely going through the motions. They appear to be good Christians, but as one writer confessed, "I was almost in all evil in the midst of the congregation" (Proverbs 5:14 KJV). You need to pray for such prodigals as much as for the openly rebellious ones. God can change them too.

Sickness

No one enjoys being sick! But when sickness forces us to step back from life, to retreat to the small world of our beds, God is with us there. He will sustain us and restore us. He may even have something He wants to teach us during this time of illness!

When we face a chronic illness, we often feel a spectrum of emotions. All these feelings are normal. We will need help coping with this condition—doctors, counselors, friends, family—but most of all, we will need to find God even here, in the midst of our illness.

Beloved, I pray that all may go well with you and that you may be in good health, as it goes well with your soul.

3 JOHN 1:2 ESV

Blessed be the God and Father of our Lord Jesus Christ, the Father of mercies and God of all comfort, who comforts us in all our affliction, so that we may be able to comfort those who are in any affliction, with the comfort with which we ourselves are comforted by God.

2 CORINTHIANS 1:3–4 ESV

To every thing there is a season, and a time to every purpose under the heaven.

ECCLESIASTES 3:1 KJV

He gives strength to the weary and increases the power of the weak. Even youths grow tired and weary, and young men stumble and fall; but those who hope in the LORD will renew their strength. They will soar on wings like eagles; they will run and not grow weary, they will walk and not be faint.

ISAIAH 40:29–31 NIV

*The Lᴏʀᴅ sustains them on their sickbed and
restores them from their bed of illness.*
PSALM 41:3 NIV

The human spirit can endure in sickness.
PROVERBS 18:14 NIV

*For He will tell His angels to care for you and keep you
in all your ways. They will hold you up in their hands.*
PSALM 91:11–12 NLV

*Pleasant words are as an honeycomb, sweet
to the soul, and health to the bones.*
PROVERBS 16:24 KJV

*Is anyone among you sick? Let him call for the elders of
the church, and let them pray over him, anointing him
with oil in the name of the Lord. And the prayer of faith
will save the sick, and the Lord will raise him up.*
JAMES 5:14–15 NKJV

*"For I know the plans I have for you," says the Lord,
"plans for well-being and not for trouble,
to give you a future and a hope."*
JEREMIAH 29:11 NLV

*"Heal the sick in it [a town] and say to them,
'The kingdom of God has come near to you.'"*
LUKE 10:9 ESV

*And God shall wipe away all tears from their eyes; and there
shall be no more death, neither sorrow, nor crying, neither shall
there be any more pain: for the former things are passed away.*
REVELATION 21:4 KJV

*But if the Spirit of Him who raised Jesus from the dead dwells
in you, He who raised Christ from the dead will also give life
to your mortal bodies through His Spirit who dwells in you.*
ROMANS 8:11 NKJV

A cheerful heart is good medicine.
PROVERBS 17:22 NIV

*Woe to me because of my injury! My wound is incurable! Yet
I said to myself, "This is my sickness, and I must endure it."*
JEREMIAH 10:19 NIV

*For our light affliction, which is but for a moment, is working
for us a far more exceeding and eternal weight of glory.*
2 CORINTHIANS 4:17 NKJV

"But for you who fear my name, the sun of righteousness shall rise with healing in its wings."

MALACHI 4:2 ESV

He himself bore our sins in his body on the tree, that we might die to sin and live to righteousness. By his wounds you have been healed.

1 PETER 2:24 ESV

He who lives in the safe place of the Most High will be in the shadow of the All-powerful. I will say to the Lord, "You are my safe and strong place, my God, in Whom I trust." For it is He Who takes you away from the trap, and from the killing sickness. He will cover you with His wings. And under His wings you will be safe. He is faithful like a safe-covering and a strong wall.

PSALM 91:1–4 NLV

God, I know that every circumstance can lead us to You, even sickness. I pray that You would use this time of pain and illness for Your greater glory.

STAYING HEALTHY

Some of you were sick because you'd lived a bad
life, your bodies feeling the effects of your sin.
PSALM 107:17 MSG

Some people believe that all illnesses are caused by sin. If they suffer a stomach ailment, it is because they failed to tithe. If they have arthritis, it is because they spoke unkindly to someone. Certainly medical conditions can have spiritual and psychosomatic roots. However, people bring most sickness on themselves by their lifestyle choices. Those who overeat and don't exercise are at a high risk of heart disease. People who have a steady diet of junk food are prone to plugged arteries and a plethora of other illnesses. And if they abuse their bodies with alcohol or tobacco, they are in danger of liver disease and cancer.

God has set up this physical world to operate according to very practical rules. Violate those rules and you will bring trouble on yourself. "You realize, don't you, that you are the temple of God. . . ? No one will get by with vandalizing God's temple, you can be sure of that" (1 Corinthians 3:17 MSG). Take care of your body. You will be glad you did.

GOD RESTORES YOUR HEALTH

*Whenever we're sick and in bed, GOD becomes
our nurse, nurses us back to health.*

PSALM 41:3 MSG

God often heals His children, but we frequently take it for granted. Think of the powers of healing God has given your body. Time and again when you are sick or injured, your body is restored to health. Each time it happens, it is a miracle of His creative power. And many times when a sickness or injury is beyond your body's ability to heal, God supernaturally intervenes and reaches out to mend you.

Some Christians believe that the New Testament's emphasis on healing is a thing of the past, while others believe that Christians today can still lay claim to healing. God is still God, and He can and does heal.

"[God] forgives all your iniquities. . .heals all your diseases" (Psalm 103:3 NKJV). God still forgives all your sins, and there is no reason that He can't still heal. Of course, He doesn't act every time you want Him to. And He may allow you to be sick for quite some time. But you can be thankful for the times He does heal.

PROTECTED FROM ILLNESS

"You must serve only the LORD your God.
If you do. . .I will protect you from illness."
EXODUS 23:25 NLT

God has made many promises in His Word to heal sickness and to protect you from getting sick. This verse explains one of the main conditions—you must wholeheartedly serve God.

You may wonder, *Doesn't Mark 11:24 say that all I need is faith? If I have enough faith I'll receive whatever I ask for—including protection from illness.* Certainly you do need faith, but there are conditions. The apostle John wrote, "Whatsoever we ask, we receive of him, because we keep his commandments, and do those things that are pleasing in his sight" (1 John 3:22 KJV).

It's a lot better to be obedient and avoid getting sick in the first place than it is to get sick and need healing. And much of staying healthy comes from obeying simple, commonsense rules, such as eating healthily.

You may still get sick from time to time, even if you are obedient, but God has promised, "Many are the afflictions of the righteous, but the LORD delivers him out of them all" (Psalm 34:19 NKJV).

SICK A LONG TIME

One of the men lying there had
been sick for thirty-eight years.
JOHN 5:5 NLT

When you read the Gospels and see how often Jesus healed people, you get an idea of how many people were sick, had disabilities, or were suffering from infirmities. A huge percentage of society was sick, and some people had suffered chronic illnesses most of their lives. Think of the man at the Pool of Bethesda. He had been bedridden for thirty-eight years.

The world's population is much greater today, and the number of sick people is also much greater. Chances are good that you know several people who suffer long-term illnesses or disabilities. The fact is, even churches who believe in healing have members who suffer on an ongoing basis.

Thank God when He heals people. And thank God for modern medicine that can also alleviate much suffering. But sometimes people suffer for years without a great deal of relief.

You really have to admire some people for how they manage to cope with limited health. They have learned both patience and humility. And while they long to be healed, they maintain a positive attitude through their condition.

THE MENDING PROCESS

"For he wounds, but he also binds up;
he injures, but his hands also heal."

JOB 5:18 NIV

For a surgeon to remedy a serious condition, he has to first cut someone open. Then he can remove a tumor, fix a hernia, or repair a heart. Once he is done, he sews up the incision. He creates a wound, but only for the purpose of healing. It's a painful but necessary part of the healing process.

God often works the same way. Even though "he does not willingly bring affliction or grief to anyone" (Lamentations 3:33 NIV), He sometimes causes pain because, as He explains, "Those whom I love I rebuke and discipline" (Revelation 3:19 NIV).

God is the Great Physician, and He acts with great wisdom, skill, and love in everything He does. Even though it may sometimes look like He hasn't successfully resolved your problems, "we know that all things work together for good to those who love God" (Romans 8:28 NKJV). Even if you have postoperative pain, it is just part of the healing process.

Be thankful for life-saving surgery, even if later it takes you a while to mend.

JESUS ALSO SUFFERED

He was despised and rejected by mankind,
a man of suffering, and familiar with pain.
ISAIAH 53:3 NIV

When you suffer from chronic pain, it is easy to think that God is distant and uncaring. Like David, you may ask, "Why do You stand afar off, O LORD? Why do You hide in times of trouble?" (Psalm 10:1 NKJV). But God knows what you are going through. He says, "I know their sorrows" (Exodus 3:7 NKJV).

The Bible calls Jesus "a man of suffering, and familiar with pain." He suffered unbelievable pain during the hours He endured scourging and crucifixion. But Jesus had suffered grief and psychological pain for years. "He came to his own people, and even they rejected him" (John 1:11 NLT). He frequently lamented, "O faithless and perverse generation, how long. . . .shall I bear with you?" (Matthew 17:17 NKJV), and He was "grieved for the hardness of their hearts" (Mark 3:5 KJV).

Jesus was "familiar with pain," and this is not merely an expression. He understands what constant suffering is like, and He will be with you in your pain and lonely hours when no one else seems to care.

FOCUSED ON PAIN

They feel but the pain of their own bodies
and mourn only for themselves.

JOB 14:22 NIV

Job was speaking for millions of people when he said, "They feel but the pain of their own bodies and mourn only for themselves." Most people who experience chronic pain are focused on their own suffering. And this is to be expected. When you are in constant discomfort and pain, you may find it difficult to concentrate on anything else.

You may be aware that many other people in this world are suffering as much as you—some even more so—but may feel you have enough to think about already, just dealing with your own misery. No one should judge you for thinking that way if you are experiencing chronic pain.

On the other hand, your suffering should give you compassion for others who are suffering also. You of all people know how they feel and are in a position to comfort them, as well as to give them advice to alleviate their pain. So reach out today to someone who, like you, is suffering. That person will appreciate it, and it will do your heart good.

Toxic Friendships

Often toxic friendships can creep up on us. We may not realize how unhealthy and poisonous a relationship has become until the problem is bigger than we know how to handle. Even once we recognize the problem, we may not know what to do.

God never wants us to be involved in something that isn't healthy for us, though. When we find ourselves involved in a toxic friendship, we need to ask Him to show us the way to freedom—for our sake, for the sake of our friend, and for His sake as well. He is not glorified by a relationship that damages and destroys!

My son, if sinners entice you, do not consent.
PROVERBS 1:10 NKJV

Happy is the man who does not walk in the way sinful men tell him to, or stand in the path of sinners, or sit with those who laugh at the truth. But he finds joy in the Law of the Lord and thinks about His Law day and night. This man is like a tree planted by rivers of water, which gives its fruit at the right time and its leaf never dries up. Whatever he does will work out well for him.
PSALM 1:1–3 NLV

Do not be deceived: "Bad company ruins good morals."
1 CORINTHIANS 15:33 ESV

A perverse person stirs up conflict, and a gossip separates close friends.
PROVERBS 16:28 NIV

Do not make friends with a hot-tempered person, do not associate with one easily angered, or you may learn their ways and get yourself ensnared.
PROVERBS 22:24–25 NIV

A friend loveth at all times,
and a brother is born for adversity.
PROVERBS 17:17 KJV

My children, let no one lead you in the wrong way. The man
who does what is right, is right with God in the same way
as Christ is right with God. The person who keeps on sinning
belongs to the devil. The devil has sinned from the beginning.
But the Son of God came to destroy the works of the devil.
1 JOHN 3:7–8 NLV

Leave the presence of a fool, for there you
do not meet words of knowledge.
PROVERBS 14:7 ESV

But avoid foolish controversies and genealogies and
arguments and quarrels about the law, because these are
unprofitable and useless. Warn a divisive person once,
and then warn them a second time. After that, have
nothing to do with them. You may be sure that such people
are warped and sinful; they are self-condemned.
TITUS 3:9–11 NIV

"And if your right hand causes you to sin, cut it off and cast it from you; for it is more profitable for you that one of your members perish, than for your whole body to be cast into hell."

MATTHEW 5:30 NKJV

Whoever walks with the wise becomes wise,
but the companion of fools will suffer harm.

PROVERBS 13:20 ESV

Be ye not unequally yoked together with unbelievers: for what fellowship hath righteousness with unrighteousness? and what communion hath light with darkness?

2 CORINTHIANS 6:14 KJV

Lord, give me wisdom to recognize when a friendship is no longer healthy. I know that true friends support one another. They accept one another. They reflect Your love to one another. When I find myself involved in a relationship that doesn't have these qualities, give me the courage to make a change.

SWAYED BY PEER PRESSURE

"You must not follow the crowd in doing wrong."
EXODUS 23:2 NLT

When you hear the words *peer pressure*, do you envision a teenager being urged by friends to commit an act of vandalism or to use drugs? The fact is, all ages are tempted to go along with a crowd. Think of coworkers trying to persuade you to help yourself to goods at your workplace or urging you to cheat on your taxes because "everyone does it."

God knows that the pressure to go along with the majority can be intense. You don't want to be a goody-goody. And you don't want to be persecuted by your workmates. Nevertheless, God commands you to buck the pressure and do what is right.

If you have been going along with the crowd and compromising your principles, you can stop doing it today. Approach the people pressuring you and tell them that your conscience won't allow you to continue. You have to do what's right. Pray for God to give you wisdom and a nonconfrontational approach. Then, if you have to lose their "friendship" over it, that is the way it has to be.

NAGGING AND MANIPULATING

She kept at it day after day, nagging and tormenting him.
JUDGES 16:16 MSG

Some people are experts at getting what they want. What they lack in logical arguments or in persuasive ability, they make up for with sheer nagging skills. They know that if they continue whining, throwing tantrums, and insisting, you will often give in.

You may have a friend like that. She manipulates you by subjecting you to an emotional roller coaster ride—at times threatening, then cajoling, then ranting, then laying guilt trips. If you are involved in such a friendship, it is wise to distance yourself from that person.

Sometimes, however, the nag is a family member whom you can't avoid. Solomon said, "A nagging spouse is like the drip, drip, drip of a leaky faucet; you can't turn it off, and you can't get away from it" (Proverbs 27:15–16 MSG).

So what do you do? You must learn to be firm with your decisions and remind the offender that she is nagging. This will, of course, upset the nag, but eventually she will give up. But you must stand your ground. After all, you can't always give in to nagging.

Unforgiveness

It's not always easy to forgive. If we are Christ's followers, however, we must follow His example. If He could forgive the people who were killing Him, we can certainly find a way to forgive those who hurt us!

Ultimately, when we can't forgive, we hurt ourselves more than anyone. Nursing a grudge damages our own hearts. It can even make us physically ill.

God wants to set us free from old grievances and harbored resentments. He will heal our wounded hearts and give us the strength to forgive. After all, He forgave us!

*Then Jesus said, "Father, forgive them,
for they do not know what they do."*

LUKE 23:34 NKJV

*For if you forgive other people when they sin against you,
your heavenly Father will also forgive you. But if you do not
forgive others their sins, your Father will not forgive your sins.*

MATTHEW 6:14–15 NIV

*If you forgive a man, I forgive him also.
If I have forgiven anything, I have done it
because of you. Christ sees me as I forgive.*

2 CORINTHIANS 2:10 NLV

*Then Peter came up and said to him, "Lord, how often
will my brother sin against me, and I forgive him?
As many as seven times?" Jesus said to him, "I do not
say to you seven times, but seventy-seven times."*

MATTHEW 18:21–22 ESV

*If anyone has caused grief, he has not so much grieved me as
he has grieved all of you to some extent—not to put it too
severely. The punishment inflicted on him by the majority
is sufficient. Now instead, you ought to forgive and comfort
him, so that he will not be overwhelmed by excessive sorrow.
I urge you, therefore, to reaffirm your love for him.*

2 CORINTHIANS 2:5–8 NIV

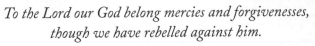

To the Lord our God belong mercies and forgivenesses,
though we have rebelled against him.
DANIEL 9:9 KJV

But I say unto you, That ye resist not evil: but whosoever shall
smite thee on thy right cheek, turn to him the other also.
MATTHEW 5:39 KJV

The discretion of a man makes him slow to anger,
and his glory is to overlook a transgression.
PROVERBS 19:11 NKJV

You must be kind to each other. Think of the other
person. Forgive other people just as God forgave
you because of Christ's death on the cross.
EPHESIANS 4:32 NLV

We forgive so that Satan will not win.
We know how he works!
2 CORINTHIANS 2:11 NLV

Bear with each other and forgive one another if any of you has
a grievance against someone. Forgive as the Lord forgave you.
COLOSSIANS 3:13 NIV

Wherefore I say unto thee, Her sins, which are
many, are forgiven; for she loved much: but to
whom little is forgiven, the same loveth little.
LUKE 7:47 KJV

" 'And should not you have had mercy on your fellow servant, as I had mercy on you?' And in anger his master delivered him to the jailers, until he should pay all his debt. So also my heavenly Father will do to every one of you, if you do not forgive your brother from your heart."

MATTHEW 18:33–35 ESV

"And whenever you stand praying, forgive, if you have anything against anyone, so that your Father also who is in heaven may forgive you your trespasses."

MARK 11:25 ESV

"Judge not, and you shall not be judged. Condemn not, and you shall not be condemned. Forgive, and you will be forgiven."

LUKE 6:37 NKJV

Our Father which art in heaven, Hallowed be thy name. Thy kingdom come. Thy will be done, as in heaven, so in earth. Give us day by day our daily bread. And forgive us our sins; for we also forgive every one that is indebted to us.

LUKE 11:2–4 KJV

God, I know You want me to live at peace with others—
but I won't be able to do that until I can forgive. Help
me forgive that which seems unforgivable. Free my
heart so that I can be at peace with everyone.

346

REASONS TO FORGIVE

*"If you do not forgive others their sins, your
Father will not forgive your sins."*
MATTHEW 6:15 NIV

When someone deliberately offends you, takes advantage of you, gossips about you, or harms you, God understands how hurt you feel. He also knows that it is a common reaction to want the other person to feel pain in return.

But only God can administer justice perfectly. So the Bible says, "Do not take revenge, my dear friends, but leave room for God's wrath, for it is written: 'It is mine to avenge; I will repay,' says the Lord" (Romans 12:19 NIV). Not taking matters into your own hands but instead trusting God to make things right takes faith.

God is well able to do that, but He needs you to unhook your fingers from the offense and give Him room to work. He even needs you to refrain from praying for vengeance and to forgive the offending party. After all, you have committed offenses yourself. "Lord, if you kept a record of our sins, who, O Lord, could ever survive?" (Psalm 130:3 NLT).

God forgives you. . .if you forgive others.

A REASON TO FORGIVE

Be ye kind one to another, tenderhearted, forgiving one another, even as God for Christ's sake hath forgiven you.

EPHESIANS 4:32 KJV

God forgave all your sins, not because you deserved it—you didn't—but because of Christ's death on the cross.

For this reason, the Bible says that you also should forgive others who have hurt or offended you. Again, you don't do this because these people *deserve* to be forgiven—they probably don't—but because you are motivated by love. "For the love of Christ compels us" (2 Corinthians 5:14 NKJV). You are to forgive others the same way that God forgave you.

God is aware when others maliciously hurt you or use you, and He is not saying that what they do should simply be excused or overlooked because they are only human. But what He does ask you to do is to forgive—even though they are guilty.

You should especially be tenderhearted toward fellow Christians. You are to live in love, "forgiving one another, if anyone has a complaint against another; even as Christ forgave you, so you also must do" (Colossians 3:13 NKJV). If you do this, God will bless you richly.

FORGIVENESS IS
SERIOUS BUSINESS

*"This is how my heavenly Father will treat each of you
unless you forgive your brother or sister from your heart."*
MATTHEW 18:35 NIV

God knows that if you have been deeply offended or wounded, it takes time to process the pain, release it to Him, and forgive the person who hurt you. But in the end, you must forgive.

Jesus told a parable about a master who forgave his servant an enormous debt. However, the servant then seized a fellow servant who owed him a small sum and threw him in jail. Angrily, the master asked, "Shouldn't you have had mercy on your fellow servant just as I had on you?" (Matthew 18:33 NIV). Then he ordered the first servant to be put in prison.

Jesus warned that God would treat believers the same way if they didn't forgive others. You must forgive others who have offended you, knowing that you yourself have been forgiven for many offenses.

God has had great mercy on you and continues to shower you with compassion. If you are filled with His love and walking in His Spirit, you will love those who have offended you and show them mercy as well.

WHY WE MUST FORGIVE

*"Forgive us our debts, as we
also have forgiven our debtors."*
MATTHEW 6:12 NIV

You may not feel a need to forgive others, but when you are in need of forgiveness, you are desperate for God to forgive. But there is a catch: in essence, Jesus said you should pray, "Forgive us our sins the exact same way we have forgiven those who have sinned against us."

But what if you have refused to forgive those indebted to you, who have sinned against you? The answer is clear: If you haven't forgiven others, then God is under no obligation to forgive you either. And He won't.

Some people think this is unfair. They think God should forgive them their many trespasses no matter how much bitterness and rage they have in their heart against His children. But should God forgive you if you have bitterness and anger against Him? No. "Whoever does not love their brother and sister, whom they have seen, cannot love God, whom they have not seen" (1 John 4:20 NIV). If you don't love others and forgive them, you don't love God, and God won't forgive you if you hate Him.

Violence

Violence bombards us from all directions. It comes at us on the news, in movies, and on television. Violence touches our schools and our workplaces. It's evident at the global level—and it even comes into our homes.

We may think we have no part in this violence, but Jesus calls us to examine our hearts. He reminds us that if our thoughts are full of rage and hatred, then we too nurse the roots of violence inside our very beings. He asks us instead to become His hands and feet on this earth, spreading His peace.

*Search me, O God, and know my heart: try me, and
know my thoughts: and see if there be any wicked
way in me, and lead me in the way everlasting.*

PSALM 139:23–24 KJV

*He shall redeem their soul from deceit and violence:
and precious shall their blood be in his sight.*

PSALM 72:14 KJV

*"Peace I leave with you, My peace I give to you; not
as the world gives do I give to you. Let not your
heart be troubled, neither let it be afraid."*

JOHN 14:27 NKJV

*Violence shall no more be heard in thy land, wasting
nor destruction within thy borders; but thou shalt
call thy walls Salvation, and thy gates Praise.*

ISAIAH 60:18 KJV

*Bring to an end the violence of the wicked and
make the righteous secure—you, the righteous
God who probes minds and hearts.*

PSALM 7:9 NIV

*You will keep the man in perfect peace whose mind
is kept on You, because he trusts in You.*
ISAIAH 26:3 NLV

*And what shall I more say? for the time would fail me
to tell of Gedeon, and of Barak, and of Samson, and
of Jephthae; of David also, and Samuel, and of the
prophets: who through faith subdued kingdoms, wrought
righteousness, obtained promises, stopped the mouths of
lions. Quenched the violence of fire, escaped the edge of
the sword, out of weakness were made strong, waxed
valiant in fight, turned to flight the armies of the aliens.*
HEBREWS 11:32–34 KJV

*Let the peace of Christ rule in your hearts, since as members
of one body you were called to peace. And be thankful.*
COLOSSIANS 3:15 NIV

*For to us a child is born, to us a son is given, and
the government will be on his shoulders. And
he will be called Wonderful Counselor, Mighty
God, Everlasting Father, Prince of Peace.*
ISAIAH 9:6 NIV

Whoever is pregnant with evil conceives trouble and gives birth to disillusionment. Whoever digs a hole and scoops it out falls into the pit they have made. The trouble they cause recoils on them; their violence comes down on their own heads.

PSALM 7:14–16 NIV

Lord, confuse the wicked, confound their words, for I see violence and strife in the city.

PSALM 55:9 NIV

"You have heard that it was said, 'An eye for an eye and a tooth for a tooth.' But I say to you, Do not resist the one who is evil. But if anyone slaps you on the right cheek, turn to him the other also."

MATTHEW 5:38–39 ESV

Dearly beloved, avenge not yourselves, but rather give place unto wrath: for it is written, Vengeance is mine; I will repay, saith the Lord.

ROMANS 12:19 KJV

Blessed are the peacemakers: for they shall be called the children of God.

MATTHEW 5:9 KJV

These things I have spoken unto you, that in me ye might have peace. In the world ye shall have tribulation: but be of good cheer; I have overcome the world.

JOHN 16:33 KJV

Blessed are the meek, for they will inherit the earth.

MATTHEW 5:5 NIV

Finally, brothers, rejoice. Aim for restoration, comfort one another, agree with one another, live in peace; and the God of love and peace will be with you.

2 CORINTHIANS 13:11 ESV

Lord, make me an instrument of Your peace. Where there is hatred, let me sow love. Where there is injury, pardon. Where there is doubt, faith. Where there is despair, hope. Where there is darkness, light. Where there is sadness, joy. O Divine Master, grant that I may not so much seek to be consoled as to console, to be understood as to understand, to be loved as to love. For it is in giving that we receive, it is in pardoning that we are pardoned, and it is in dying that we are born to eternal life. (Prayer of Francis of Assisi)

AVOIDING VIOLENCE

The answer's simple: Live right,
speak the truth. . .reject violence.
ISAIAH 33:15–16 MSG

When someone cuts you off in traffic, nearly causing an accident, you are understandably angry. The same is true when someone physically attacks you, vandalizes your property, or lies about you. Anger has its rightful place, but the Bible warns, "Be angry, and do not sin" (Ephesians 4:26 NKJV). Many people sin when they are angry by committing violent acts against others.

Violence can quickly spiral out of control; you might hurt someone more than you intended to and end up facing serious consequences. Plus, violence usually provokes more violence and vendettas; you create bitter enemies, and you too can end up hurt.

Psalm 7:16 (NIV) says, "The trouble they cause recoils on them; their violence comes down on their own heads." Violence is almost always a two-edged sword, hurting those who strike out as much as those they attack.

If you must take some form of action to protect yourself, be aware that there are a number of well-thought-out responses that avoid violence. Even when exercising your right to self-defense, use restraint.

LIVING BY THE SWORD

"Put away your sword," Jesus told him.
"Those who use the sword will die by the sword."
MATTHEW 26:52 NLT

Many criminals live by the sword. They pack heavy firepower, sometimes even outgunning the police. They live and die in a violent world. But many people today engage in violence, even though they don't use guns. They give vent to their anger with their fists or whatever objects they can get ahold of.

If you find yourself expressing anger with violence, seek help to manage your temper. You may have avoided doing damage thus far, but it is only a matter of time before you do something that you will regret. You may traumatize loved ones, and though you apologize afterward, the damage will have been done.

Violence will also get you in trouble with the law. Eventually, if you fail to curb your temper, it will ensure that you suffer at the hands of another violent person. If you use the sword, you will die by the sword. It will take time, but it will certainly happen.

Trust God to work out situations, and turn away from violence. This will give God the needed space to work.

A VIOLENT WORLD

*The earth also was corrupt before God, and
the earth was filled with violence.*

GENESIS 6:11 NKJV

In Noah's day the earth was a very violent place, and Jesus tells us that "as the days of Noah were, so also will the coming of the Son of Man be" (Matthew 24:37 NKJV).

Every time you watch the news, you see incidents of violence. There is a steady stream of crime in the streets, in the malls, in the schools, and in the homes of our nation. You get the impression that the hour is late for planet Earth.

But all this violence isn't just a statistic, nor is it simply a fulfillment of Bible prophecy; real crimes are being committed against real people. You yourself or a member of your family may have been a victim of violent crime and know the trauma it brings. It can leave you shaken and insecure.

But know this also: "God has not given us a spirit of fear, but of power and of love" (2 Timothy 1:7 NKJV), and "perfect love casts out fear" (2 Timothy 1:7; 1 John 4:18 NKJV). So let God fill you with His assurance and love.

Weakness

There are so many demands on our strength. So many crises to confront, so many problems to solve, so many people who need our help. We feel exhausted. We're not sure we can go on. Some days we'd like to just give up. We've reached the end of our strength.

But when we acknowledge our own weakness, that's the moment when the Holy Spirit can begin to work in our lives in new ways. When we throw up our own hands, God's hands have room to work.

But he said to me, "My grace is sufficient for you,
for my power is made perfect in weakness." Therefore
I will boast all the more gladly of my weaknesses,
so that the power of Christ may rest upon me.

2 CORINTHIANS 12:9 ESV

But they that wait upon the LORD shall renew their strength;
they shall mount up with wings as eagles; they shall run,
and not be weary; and they shall walk, and not faint.

ISAIAH 40:31 KJV

Then Peter said, "Silver or gold I do not have, but what I do
have I give you. In the name of Jesus Christ of Nazareth,
walk." Taking him by the right hand, he helped him up,
and instantly the man's feet and ankles became strong.

ACTS 3:6–7 NIV

But God chose what is foolish in the world to shame the wise;
God chose what is weak in the world to shame the strong.

1 CORINTHIANS 1:27 ESV

I long to see you so that I may impart to you some
spiritual gift to make you strong—that is, that you and
I may be mutually encouraged by each other's faith.

ROMANS 1:11–12 NIV

*And His name, through faith in His name, has made
this man strong, whom you see and know. Yes, the
faith which comes through Him has given him this
perfect soundness in the presence of you all.*
ACTS 3:16 NKJV

*I came to you in weakness with great fear and trembling.
My message and my preaching were not with wise
and persuasive words, but with a demonstration
of the Spirit's power, so that your faith might not
rest on human wisdom, but on God's power.*
1 CORINTHIANS 2:3–5 NIV

*And what more shall I say? For the time would fail me to tell
of Gideon and Barak and Samson and Jephthah, also of David
and Samuel and the prophets: who through faith subdued
kingdoms, worked righteousness, obtained promises, stopped
the mouths of lions, quenched the violence of fire, escaped
the edge of the sword, out of weakness were made strong.*
HEBREWS 11:32–34 NKJV

*I receive joy when I am weak. . . .
For when I am weak, then I am strong.*
2 CORINTHIANS 12:10 NLV

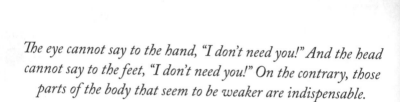

The eye cannot say to the hand, "I don't need you!" And the head cannot say to the feet, "I don't need you!" On the contrary, those parts of the body that seem to be weaker are indispensable.

1 CORINTHIANS 12:21–22 NIV

Likewise the Spirit helps us in our weakness.

ROMANS 8:26 ESV

"Everyone will be made cleaner and stronger with fire."

MARK 9:49 NLV

So is it with the resurrection of the dead. What is sown is perishable; what is raised is imperishable. It is sown in dishonor; it is raised in glory. It is sown in weakness; it is raised in power.

1 CORINTHIANS 15:42–43 ESV

My body and my heart may grow weak, but God is the strength of my heart and all I need forever.

PSALM 73:26 NLV

*For we do not have a High Priest who cannot
sympathize with our weaknesses.*
HEBREWS 4:15 NKJV

*For though He was crucified in weakness, yet He lives by
the power of God. For we also are weak in Him, but we
shall live with Him by the power of God toward you.*
2 CORINTHIANS 13:4 NKJV

Watch, stand fast in the faith, be brave, be strong.
1 CORINTHIANS 16:13 NKJV

*To the weak I became weak, to win the weak.
I have become all things to all people so that by
all possible means I might save some.*
1 CORINTHIANS 9:22 NIV

---

*Lord, You know how weak I am. But I can do all
things through You. Heavenly Father, make me strong
in You. May my strength come from Your might.*

WE ARE DUST

He knows how weak we are;
he remembers we are only dust.

PSALM 103:14 NLT

God knows how prone to failure people are. He knows that you love Him and long to serve Him, but as Jesus observed, "The spirit is willing, but the flesh is weak" (Mark 14:38 NIV).

If you are strong willed, you may be frustrated by how weak others seem, by how easily they succumb to temptation or disappoint you. You may be disappointed at how spiritually immature someone is and feel like blurting out in exasperation, "Come on! You can do better than that! Pull yourself up by your bootstraps!"

Although God Himself wishes that such people would mature faster, don't forget that He constantly has mercy on them. Just before saying that He knows how weak people are, mere dust, the Bible says, "The LORD is like a father to his children, tender and compassionate to those who fear him" (Psalm 103:13 NLT). This isn't to excuse people who are flagrantly sinning, but it is a reminder to have compassion on those who are weak in areas where you are strong.

WE ARE BUT A SHADOW

We are but of yesterday, and know nothing,
because our days upon earth are a shadow.

JOB 8:9 KJV

Compared to God, people have the lifespan of a moth. Even compared to the angels, we are just flickering shadows fleeting across the ground. We are a thin mist, quickly vanishing in the morning light.

As David prayed, "You have made my days as handbreadths, and my age is as nothing before You; certainly every man at his best state is but vapor" (Psalm 39:5 NKJV). A "handbreadth" is one of the smallest biblical measurements, only the width of a palm.

Human beings live about seventy to eighty years, which may seem like a long time, but to God it is as if we were born yesterday. Many people are just beginning to acquire wisdom and accomplish their life's objectives at that age—when their strength fails and life ends.

In the beginning, God didn't make humans so futile and weak. God designed us to be immortal. We are literally a shadow of what we were intended to be. It's good to keep this in mind when you are tempted to get proud about your beauty, your strength, or your accomplishments.

Work

Our jobs are often the source of much of the stress in our lives. Tight deadlines, multiple responsibilities, conflicts with coworkers and supervisors—all these can lead to tension. We're likely to spend about half our lives in our workplaces, though, so we need to find joy and satisfaction, rather than stress and anxiety, in our jobs.

We can learn to sense God's presence with us as we work. Even on our busiest days, we need to take time to whisper a prayer or spend a quiet moment with our Lord.

By the seventh day God had finished the work he had been doing; so on the seventh day he rested from all his work. Then God blessed the seventh day and made it holy, because on it he rested from all the work of creating that he had done.

GENESIS 2:2–3 NIV

When you eat the labor of your hands, you shall be happy, and it shall be well with you.

PSALM 128:2 NKJV

Therefore, I urge you, brothers and sisters, in view of God's mercy, to offer your bodies as a living sacrifice, holy and pleasing to God—this is your true and proper worship. Do not conform to the pattern of this world, but be transformed by the renewing of your mind. Then you will be able to test and approve what God's will is—his good, pleasing and perfect will.

ROMANS 12:1–2 NIV

The people of Israel were sad in their spirit because of being servants. They cried for help. And because of their hard work their cry went up to God. God heard their crying and remembered His agreement with Abraham, Isaac and Jacob. God saw the people of Israel and He cared about them.

EXODUS 2:23–25 NLV

"Do not work for the food that perishes, but for the food that endures to eternal life, which the Son of Man will give to you. For on him God the Father has set his seal."
JOHN 6:27 ESV

He who works with a lazy hand is poor, but the hand of the hard worker brings riches. A son who gathers in summer is wise, but a son who sleeps during gathering time brings shame.
PROVERBS 10:4–5 NLV

Whatever you do, work at it with all your heart, as working for the Lord, not for human masters, since you know that you will receive an inheritance from the Lord as a reward. It is the Lord Christ you are serving.
COLOSSIANS 3:23–24 NIV

Some good comes from all work.
PROVERBS 14:23 NLV

And I heard a voice from heaven saying, "Write this: Blessed are the dead who die in the Lord from now on." "Blessed indeed," says the Spirit, "that they may rest from their labors, for their deeds follow them!"
REVELATION 14:13 ESV

If a man works, his pay is not a gift.
It is something he has earned.
ROMANS 4:4 NLV

But we urge you, brethren, that you increase more and
more; that you also aspire to lead a quiet life, to mind
your own business, and to work with your own hands, as
we commanded you, that you may walk properly toward
those who are outside, and that you may lack nothing.
1 THESSALONIANS 4:10–12 NKJV

I glorified you on earth, having accomplished
the work that you gave me to do.
JOHN 17:4 ESV

Consider the lilies of the field, how they grow; they toil
not, neither do they spin: and yet I say unto you, That
even Solomon in all his glory was not arrayed·like one
of these. Wherefore, if God so clothe the grass of the field,
which to day is, and to morrow is cast into the oven,
shall he not much more clothe you, O ye of little faith?
MATTHEW 6:28–30 KJV

Do not be lazy but always work hard. Work for the Lord with a heart full of love for Him.
ROMANS 12:11 NLV

Yes, God kept us from what looked like sure death and He is keeping us. As we trust Him, He will keep us in the future.
2 CORINTHIANS 1:10 NLV

"Come to Me, all you who labor and are heavy laden, and I will give you rest. Take My yoke upon you and learn from Me, for I am gentle and lowly in heart, and you will find rest for your souls. For My yoke is easy and My burden is light."
MATTHEW 11:28–30 NKJV

Heavenly Lord, thank You for my job. May I be challenged and inspired by the work I do. Even in the midst of stress, even on the days when I fail, may I look away from my own feelings and see You—and beyond You, a world that needs my efforts, no matter how small they may seem. Give me the will and strength to work hard today. May I find gladness in my efforts, and most of all, may I please You.

ENDURING PROLONGED
UNEMPLOYMENT

*"Keep on asking, and you will receive what you
ask for. Keep on seeking, and you will find."*
MATTHEW 7:7 NLT

You may have been out of work so long that you have almost
given up on finding employment. Or you may be working
part time for low wages. So you pray for God to change
your situation. But when the drought continues, you may be
tempted to give up.

In Elijah's day, Israel suffered from drought. After three
and a half years, Elijah prayed for God to send rain. Then
he told his servant to go look toward the sea. The servant
returned, saying that he didn't see anything. Again Elijah
prayed. Again he sent his servant. After doing this seven
times, the servant finally saw a storm cloud.

Soon rain was falling heavily. The drought was over. But
it didn't happen the first time Elijah prayed. He had to pray
persistently before God answered (see 1 Kings 18:42–45).
Jesus said that "men ought always to pray, and not to faint"
(Luke 18:1 KJV).

So don't stop praying! You may have to wait awhile, but
God will answer your prayers.

WORK AS UNTO THE LORD

Work willingly at whatever you do, as though you
were working for the Lord rather than for people.
COLOSSIANS 3:23 NLT

One of the most common sources of stress on the job is
having a boss you don't like. Some bosses seem to have the
idea that since they are boss, they can be blunt and incon-
siderate, and their workers have to put up with them or be
put out the door. Even bosses who are more considerate and
reasonable still may do things that irk you.

The Bible has a solution: If you can't change your boss's
attitude, change your own. Work as if you are working for
Jesus, not for imperfect people. Peter advised, "Submit
yourselves to your masters, not only to those who are good
and considerate, but also to those who are harsh" (1 Peter
2:18 NIV). He was writing this to slaves, and some had truly
harsh masters.

For the last two thousand years, this advice has helped
countless believers put up with unpleasant work—and not
only survive, but thrive.

If you simply can't stand your boss, the best option might
be to look for a new job.

A HEAVY WORKLOAD

"We are unworthy servants who have simply done our duty."
LUKE 17:10 NLT

You shouldn't expect lavish praise for doing what you are paid to do. And while a good boss will comment when you do your job competently, he or she is not obliged to do so. Praise is only due when you go beyond the call of duty.

Where work stress can come in is when your boss regularly requires you to do more than your job description. If you protest, you may be told that many people would be happy to have your job. And that may be true.

Now, you can carry the extra load for some time, but after a while the stress will get to you. Either that or you will need a fresh source of strength to buoy you up. That's where you must look to the Lord.

Jesus spoke to overworked laborers, saying, "Come unto me, all ye that labour and are heavy laden, and I will give you rest. Take my yoke upon you. . .and ye shall find rest unto your souls" (Matthew 11:28–29 KJV). Having spiritual peace can even help you carry a demanding workload.

Worry

Guess what the Old German root word of *worry* means. It means "to strangle"! Worries strangle us. They hinder our ability to breathe in the Spirit of God. Worries interfere with the flow of God's life into ours.

But our worries can be turned into prayers. Each time a worry occurs to us, we need to form the habit of lifting it up to God. As we offer our worries to Him, they will lose their stranglehold on our lives. And then we will find ourselves instead thanking God for all He has done.

*Do not worry. Learn to pray about everything. Give
thanks to God as you ask Him for what you need.*
PHILIPPIANS 4:6 NLV

*"Therefore I tell you, do not worry about your life, what you
will eat or drink; or about your body, what you will wear.
Is not life more than food, and the body more than clothes?"*
MATTHEW 6:25 NIV

*"Can any one of you by worrying add
a single hour to your life?"*
MATTHEW 6:27 NIV

*My soul also is greatly troubled; but You, O L*ORD—
*how long? Return, O L*ORD*, deliver me!*
PSALM 6:3–4 NKJV

*Do not worry yourself because of those who do wrong, and
do not be jealous of the sinful. For there will be no future
for the sinful man. The lamp of the sinful will be put out.*
PROVERBS 24:19–20 NLV

"The seed that fell among thorns stands for those who hear, but as they go on their way they are choked by life's worries, riches and pleasures, and they do not mature. But the seed on good soil stands for those with a noble and good heart, who hear the word, retain it, and by persevering produce a crop."

LUKE 8:14–15 NIV

"But blessed is the one who trusts in the LORD, whose confidence is in him. They will be like a tree planted by the water that sends out its roots by the stream. It does not fear when heat comes; its leaves are always green. It has no worries in a year of drought and never fails to bear fruit."

JEREMIAH 17:7–8 NIV

And Jesus answered and said unto her, Martha, Martha, thou art careful and troubled about many things: but one thing is needful: and Mary hath chosen that good part, which shall not be taken away from her.

LUKE 10:41–42 KJV

"Therefore do not worry about tomorrow,
for tomorrow will worry about its own things.
Sufficient for the day is its own trouble."
MATTHEW 6:34 NKJV

Do not fret because of those who are evil. . . . Trust in the
Lord and do good; dwell in the land and enjoy safe pasture.
Take delight in the Lord, and he will give you the desires of
your heart. Commit your way to the Lord; trust in him and
he will do this: He will make your righteous reward shine like
the dawn, your vindication like the noonday sun. Be still before
the Lord and wait patiently for him; do not fret when people
succeed in their ways, when they carry out their wicked schemes.
PSALM 37:1, 3–7 NIV

When my worry is great within me,
Your comfort brings joy to my soul.
PSALM 94:19 NLV

"Do not worry about the things that belong to you.
For the best of all the land of Egypt is yours."
GENESIS 45:20 NLV

"But when they deliver you up, do not worry about
how or what you should speak. For it will be given
to you in that hour what you should speak."

MATTHEW 10:19 NKJV

*Let not your heart be troubled: ye believe in God, believe also
in me. In my Father's house are many mansions: if it were
not so, I would have told you. I go to prepare a place for you.
And if I go and prepare a place for you, I will come again, and
receive you unto myself; that where I am, there ye may be also.*

JOHN 14:1–3 KJV

Give all your worries to Him because He cares for you.

1 PETER 5:7 NLV

---

*Thank You, Father, for giving me the confidence that You are
for me and with me. I know that life holds nothing that You
can't overcome. No power is greater than You. I can rest in Your
arms today, knowing that You have everything under control.*

GIVE GOD YOUR WORRIES

Give all your worries and cares to God, for he cares about you.
1 PETER 5:7 NLT

Everyone worries from time to time, but some people are especially prone to it. Whichever category you fall into—but especially if you are a constant worrier—God's solution is to give Him all your cares. Why? Because a constant state of anxiety isn't good for your mental or physical health. Psalm 37:8 (NKJV) says, "Do not fret—it only causes harm."

There are two more reasons why you should hand all your worries and cares to God. The first is that He genuinely cares about you and doesn't want you to suffer needlessly. Knowing the human tendency to want to try and sort everything out, He made it a command: "Give all your worries and cares to God."

The second reason is that God is all powerful and is, in fact, the only one in existence capable of resolving all your problems.

"Let us therefore come boldly unto the throne of grace," lay the problem at His feet, and trust Him to "help in time of need" (Hebrews 4:16 KJV).

WORRYING IS USELESS

"Can any one of you by worrying
add a single hour to your life?"

MATTHEW 6:27 NIV

Not only can you not add one hour to your life by worrying but worry will probably cut years from your life. Anxiety, prolonged over time, has a negative effect on your health, leading to insomnia, stomach disorders, and—in worst-case scenarios—heart attacks.

Jesus warned that stress would be a major killer in the last days, with "men's hearts failing them from fear" (Luke 21:26 NKJV). So worrying is not only useless, it is worse than useless and highly detrimental.

So many people worry about trivial things. Yet Jesus admonished you not even to worry about vitally important things. He said, "Therefore do not worry, saying, 'What shall we eat?' or 'What shall we drink?' or 'What shall we wear?'" (Matthew 6:31 NKJV).

Certainly God expects you to work to provide the money you need to live, so He is not advising you to be lazy or complacent. But He commands you not to worry. Even if your financial situation is unstable, you do well to remember that God is your Ultimate Provider.

ONE DAY AT A TIME

"Do not worry about tomorrow, for tomorrow will worry about itself. Each day has enough trouble of its own."
MATTHEW 6:34 NIV

Jesus warned against the futility of worrying about the future, focusing on trouble that hasn't even happened yet. Doing so distracts you from important things you should concentrate on today.

Certainly if there are large events or problems looming on the horizon—for example, if you are responsible to organize a banquet—you can't ignore giving thought to them. But you are simply to make whatever plans you can then commit the unresolved details to God in prayer, not worry about them.

The difference between *planning for* tomorrow and *worrying about* tomorrow is that worrying often involves getting your eyes on the entire problem at once, then despairing that you can't handle it; whereas planning means having the faith that you can meet the challenge if you pray and take practical steps to meet it.

When Jesus said that today already has enough troubles that require your attention, He was basically advising you to keep your eyes on God, moment by moment, not on your problems.

WORRY WEIGHS YOU DOWN

Worry weighs us down; a cheerful word picks us up.
PROVERBS 12:25 MSG

If you are concerned about your finances, your health, a wayward child, a relationship, or any number of other things, you will be tempted to worry. This is especially true if the situation looks difficult and things stand a very real chance of not working out in your favor.

At times like that, a cheerful word can encourage you. It doesn't even have to be the total solution to your problems, such as, "The check just arrived!" or "The test came back negative!" It can simply be a cheerful word, someone letting you know that someone cares—because that lets you know that *God* cares.

The reason this can be so encouraging is that although you would like God to resolve things at once, your immediate need is to know that God sees your situation, cares, and will be coming through for you. This is why David prayed, "Send me a sign of your favor. . . . For you, O Lord, help and comfort me" (Psalm 86:17 NLT).

This is also a good reason to be sure to comfort and encourage others.

FIND STRENGTH IN TALKING
TO GOD IN DIFFICULT TIMES

199 Encouraging Prayers for Difficult Times

Here's a practical and encouraging book containing 199 short prayer starters that will help you pray confidently during difficult times.

Paperback / 978-1-63609-007-8 / $4.99

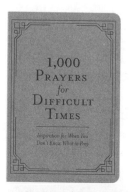

1,000 Prayers for Difficult Times

Here's a practical and encouraging book containing 1,000 short prayer starters that will help you pray confidently during difficult times.

DiCarta / 978-1-68322-723-6 / $15.99

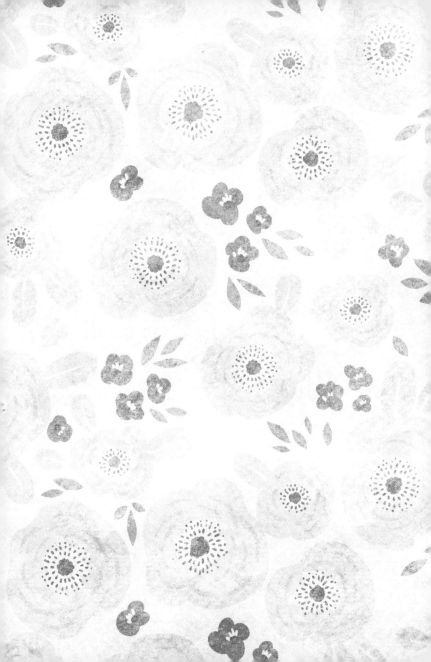